Preface

The worst nightmare any parent can face is to be told that their child has died. Immediately your whole world is thrown into darkness; your head becomes light and your brain ceases to function. All at once it becomes too much to comprehend and the world begins to spin.

Every question conceivable begins to flood your mind; how, where, when and why? All the questions that you cannot find answers to in your brain begin to overpower your mind. At once you begin to call on God and pray that the message you got is a mistake, that they have called the wrong parent; but it is not so, your child is gone.

The questions remain; what happened; where did it happen how did it happen and why did it happen? And the biggest question of all; where is my child now?

This book is not all about our son but how we coped with our tragedy. In this book you will find many answers to your questions. Answers that finally gave us blessed peace, in our hearts and with God. The answers will change your life and the way you see our loving Father in Heaven.

Remember this: He too lost His son for a while on the cross. He too felt His heart being ripped out of his chest. And if you think He does not understand your pain: you are very wrong, for He does. Therefore, He can comfort you in many ways you do not think possible.

My Father in Heaven can see right into your heart, He can feel your pain, He cries with you, but most of all, He takes you in his arm and comforts you and directs you to look in His Word for answers to your questions.

The healing process is not quick by any means. Grieving is all part of the healing process. But how do we heal? That is the question this book addresses.

For young parents raising small children, this book helps one to realise the importance of correct upbringing. Mothers and fathers do not receive a manual at the birth of their child on how to raise their baby. This is putting it roughly: "look mom, dad, you have a healthy baby, now see to it that you feed and clothe him or her." What do I read to my child, what do I teach my child; will my baby become a criminal or a good citizen?

Well you can be at ease, the answer is in this book, for this is the way we raised our children and because of that, we know where our son is today, regardless of his reason for taking his own life. We have no doubt in our minds, and so will you after reading how God showed us where he is today. God's word is truth.

Many aspects of healing are covered in these pages; all used by professional people in their field. Many quotations have been used as guides to help you heal, don't feel that you are not making progress when you breakdown and cry; it is your love for your child that does that and it is cathartic to cry. You will never not cry over your child, never. They were part of you and will be until the day you go to your rest. You will think of a moment spent with them, a very specific moment that brought you joy, and the tears will flow like a river. My wife and I still do, and we comfort each other.

Our strength lies in the promises of our Lord Jesus Christ, and at the end of this book, so might yours.

God bless you from Ken and Jennifer as you start teaching your children how to cope with life and for you who are as we are, may our Father in Heaven embrace you in His arms.

Lord, Remember Me.

<u>Part 1</u>

Finally; a day of licentious revelry and sincere thanks to their god had arrived. It was the first time in years that the Philistines had been able to come to their god, Dagon, with hearts of praise. How they had suffered these many years under the yoke of that Nazarene. One man, who terrorized their people, and slew them by the hundreds, making it known that it was through his God that he was able to destroy them and that while they worshiped a counterfeit god, he would keep on at them. How they hated him, seeking ways both day and night to destroy him.

Then his eyes fell on Delilah, oh how she pleased him. Seeing his delight, the Philistine lords came to her to find his weakness so that they might prevail against him. Her soft skin, sweet smelling cent dulled his sense of reason, soon she learned of his secret, his true weakness.

Asleep, trusting in her, for he loved her; she called for the lords and a man to come in and shaved off his seven locks of hair. When he awoke, he found that her love for him was false, his strength gone, and so was she.

Powerless to engage his captors, he was taken to a place, there his eyes were put out after which he was carried away down to Gaza. There he was blinded, bound in fetters and brass to a grinder in the prison house.

The streets rang with jubilation, men, women and children, all extravagantly dressed, waving banners, shouting praise to their god Dagon. Young maidens danced, shook their tambourines while others sounded symbols and sang songs as they made their way to the great temple house.

Thousands poured into and onto the roof of this great temple to see and give praise to their idol Dagon. In the centre of the great house, sports of many kinds were being displayed to entertain the worshipers. The heart of the arena, spoiled by the blood of slaves that fell under the swords of the gladiators soon lost its appeal. Their hearts merry with wine, their bellies filled with meats of diverse kinds and the morning almost reaching its meridian, the lord and ladies became uninterested in the field events and wanted something more exciting, something more exhilarating to fill their insatiable eyes.

"My lord, why do we not call for Samson, surely he would bring cheer to the crowds?"

"Yes, yes the mighty Samson, why not." Chuckled all the other ladies whilst sipping wine.

"Let him come and entertain us with sport, send for him at once." commanded the lords and priests of the temple, as they raised their chalices and called for more wine.

The trumpets sounded and the cry went out for all to hear that Samson was to come and make sport.

In the prison house, the prisoners and Samson could hear the cheers go up from the crowd as they called out his name repeatedly, Samson, Samson, Samson. Cheated by Delilah; blinded by the hands of his enemy, and for many-a-day grinding in the prison house, he now waited for the jailer to come and undo his chains to be led to the house of Dagon for sport. The once mighty Samson was led away like a child to make sport for his captors.

Soon they too tired of him; he was led to stand by two pillars. He could feel the sun's rays on his face as he lifted his head, the cool breeze on his brow, the locks of hair on his shoulder moved within the gentle wind. Unable to see where he was, he asked the boy with him to let him feel the two main arch pillars upon which the house was built. The lad took Samson's strong hands in his small hands and led him and placed him between them.

Samson reached out and touched them. Feeling sure of his stance between them he asked the boy "Are these the two pillars that the house stands on?"

The boy stood next to Samson, looked up at him and said "Yes, these are they."

Samson placed his hands firmly on the pillars and said to the lad "Run home lad, run to your mother, run now and stay there, do not turn around, just keep running."

Samson went down on one knee and looked up, with the right hand on one pillar and the left hand on the other.

Samson knew how much he had hurt his Lord and God, he had spent hours in that prison seeking God, begging His forgiveness. He knew that he could not return to yesterday or go back into his mother womb to be born again, to avoid his mistakes. He could no longer look up at the stars and ponder the Glory of God the Creator of Heaven and earth. He had been given the task by his God to judge Israel and he failed, but would God remember him in this hour of his need?

Samson trusted in God, even if he had sinned, he knew God would not forget him. So Samson called out to God. Samson called out to the God of his fathers. Samson called out to his God, the true God. "O Lord God, remember me, I pray thee, and strengthen me, I pray thee, only this once, O God, that I may be at once avenged of the Philistines for my two eyes" And Samson took hold of the two pillars upon which the house stood, and on which it was borne up, of the one with his right hand, and of the other with his left. And Samson said "Let me die with the Philistines." And he bowed himself with all his might; and the house fell…"(Judges 16: 28-30.)

Down in that grinding house, blind, frustrated, alone with his thoughts and not knowing what was happening to his people, the people that God had given to him to judge. Samson felt so empty and rejected of God, so unworthy, yet he believed in Him, trusted Him. Samson is mentioned in Hebrews 11:32, 33 (the Faith Chapter) among the saved. The emptiness of the soul is the worst emptiness any human can face, the enemy of God knows this, only by the grace of God are we saved.

The once mighty Samson, upon whom his people depended, now blinded, looked to others for sustenance and water. How he must have longed to hear his mother's voice, to listen to his father recite the book of Moses, and to break bread with them. Sitting there alone in blind darkness knowing that all that befell him was all his own doing, wondering how he could make it right with God. Praying calling on God for deliverance and forgiveness, but all he got was silence and more silence from God. Where was God, was He listening to Samson or not? We might ask this of our own children, who went before us as did Samson before his parents. Did God hear our child or children calling, did He answer them? please God help us understand, help us to find peace.

Did Samson's father ask the same questions? What went through his mind when he fetched his sons' body for burial? Did he stay close to God all the days of his life, so as to ask God on the resurrection morning, we know differently today? We know that Samson is saved; his father did not. How often did he cry out to the Lord "Did my son call upon you my Lord before his death? Did he find favour in your sight Lord?"

As parents we do not know the thoughts that went through the minds of our child or children when they pulled on the handle of life's handbrake and brought it to a standstill, but God knows, if we want to know, we must follow in His footsteps starting a close relationship with our Lord and Saviour Jesus Christ remaining faithful unto the end of life's journey.

Join my wife and me, as we await the second coming of our Saviour Jesus Christ, and to meet with our son, Lance and other loved ones we have lost. Here is our tragic, heart rendering story and how we are, through Jesus' grace and peace, coping with it. By careful study of His word, you too can find peace as we have through our Saviour Jesus Christ.

For the Biblical account of Samson's life and death; read Judges 13:24 – 25. Then chapters 14 – 16:1-31

<u>Part 2</u>

Not our son

Chapter 1

Clouds rolled lazily across the sky that cool January afternoon as we drew nearer to East London. The journey had been a lengthy one with many stops along the way. We promised our younger son that we would take rests and stretch our legs. Both my wife and I are getting on in age and long trips are starting to take their toll, so we also promised to call each time we stopped to let him know that we were okay. After a while we began to feel as if we were children reporting home to dad, it gave us something to smile about, his love for us is undeniable.

There it was, the horizon of the sea, what a relief. I wound down my window and asked my wife "Should we go past the beach before going to Owen?" I turned to take in a deep breath of air.

Jen was doing a crossword puzzle at the time but stopped and looked over at me and replied "What a question, really. We have to go past the beach first, I want to see the waves; did you even have to ask that question?" I smiled at her, the next stretch we drove in silence.

We entered East London and drove straight for the beach, all our travel fatigue abated at the sound of the waves. We parked the car and with some difficulty got out. We must have looked a sight as we were both joint bound by the long journey since our last stop. Fortunately, nobody took any notice of us as we struggled to straighten ourselves up.

We stood there on the sidewalk waiting for reality to fill our minds and reset our mood to one of relaxation. The smell of the sea, wind in our hair and faces, the sight of the break-wall and small pier, where as a young lad I spent many happy hours fishing. To our left the sandy hills and flat rocks...home at last. Even though the past approximately twenty nine years we had spent in the Gauteng, we were both born and raised right here in East London and this is our home.

After a good while of taking in the sea, Jen thought it time to go to Owen's place, we still needed to unpack and chat, believe me she and Owen can chat. As brother and sister, they have always been close. Distance was overcome by cell phones and emails. Like some young men, Owen decided to stay single and today lives alone in a large house which he opens up to us when we come down on holiday. He had not been well a few years back and Jen had spent time with him making sure he took his meds and got to the doctor.

We pulled into the driveway and hooted; Jen got out and called out to her brother. "He knows we are coming, he must be at the back."

And then he appeared from around the corner smiling broadly "Hold on, I'm coming, the key moved itself from the shelf to the table, they do that you know, just to confuse us." He waved the keys in his hand at us "But I found them."

His two large dogs were also happy to see us, after a few hugs, licks, loud deep barks and a little chit chat, I got back into the car and drove it into the yard while Owen locked the gates behind me, well trying to, with Jen hugging him and the dogs jumping up at her. Jen gave the dogs some attention and then they turned to me, oh boy, I'm not a doggy person, I like birds and tropical fish, they slobbered all over me as I carried the suitcases into the house.

With the car unpacked, locked and a mug of tea in hand, we were finally able to report to Morgan, our younger son, that we were safely in Owen's house. He was relieved saying. "Now I can relax knowing that my parentals are safe, (his pet word for us), speak to you later, love you."

Our Heavenly Father had blessed us with a safe and pleasant journey. The scenery too was green and pleasing to the eye which made the journey so much more relaxing.

Jen gave Owen an almost detailed report of our trip down, which was as exciting as it could get for an over sixty couple traveling within the speed limit and super glad when a sign appeared for a filling station which meant restrooms, yeah, toilets.

It was getting late, we were both tired so excused ourselves and went to bed, why, I do not know, all I saw when I closed my eyes were flashing white lines, but somehow my brain capitulated to the power of exhaustion for the next thing I knew it was morning.

It was late when I woke up, Jen had left me to sleep in, she had been trying to reach our eldest son Lance but to no avail, his phone just rang and rang. Jen came into the room and saw that I was awake "Why can't you guys keep your phones with you? You and Lance, never have your phone with you. How are people supposed to reach you? You should be like me and Morgan; we keep our phones with us."

I lifted my head slightly off the pillow, "Morning sweetie-pie, any tea?"

She did not even look at me, "Get up and I will make some for you" and left the room, redialling Lance's number.

I got up and changed, went through to the bath room and on my way I heard her leave a message for Lance "Hi Lance, we are here at Uncle Owen's place, please call, love mom."

I finished up in the bathroom and went back to the bedroom, Jen had just put her phone down on the dresser and was about to transfer the last few blouses to the cupboard. The first item that I had taken out of my suitcase was my Bible and put it on the table alongside my bed, as had Jen. I sat down on my side of the bed and took my Bible in hand whilst waiting for Jen to finish and join me for morning prayers. I did not kneel to pray the night before because I was so tired, my thoughts would have drifted and I feared I might fall asleep on my knees, so while lying on the bed, I thanked my Heavenly Father for the safe journey. Tiredness had crept through my body like a serpent causing me to yawn. I could not keep my eyes open. I knew that the enemy would love to shoot thoughts into my mind to distract me and that is why I prayed a short prayer.

Jen sat down beside me, we held hands and for a few moments we were silent. We had left Johannesburg with a reading from Isaiah 41:10- 13

Fear thou not; for I am with thee: be not dismayed; for I am thy God: I will strengthen thee; yea, I will help thee; yea, I will uphold thee with the right hand of my righteousness. Behold, all they that were incensed against thee shall be ashamed and confounded: they shall be as nothing; and they that strive with thee shall perish. Thou shall seek them, and shall not find them, even, them that contended with thee: they that war against thee shall be as nothing, and as a thing of naught. For I the Lord thy God will hold thy right hand, saying unto thee, Fear not; for I will help thee.

Now it was time to thank our Father for His blessings, as Jen started to read a verse to open our morning prayers, the dogs ran up the driveway over which our bedroom window looked, and began barking. We kept going, I asked God to intervene, believe it or not, the dogs ran off into the yard and we were able to continue our worship in silence. I thanked God for my children, that they were safe and healthy, I thanked God for my wife who has stood by my side all through these years as well as helping me stay alert while driving down here. I prayed for Owen, glad that he looked well, and for opening his home to us. Then we prayed for our church, ministers, missionaries, and for the TV and radio stations that were spreading the Gospel of Jesus Christ.

It is very important to us that we pray for the Gospel of Jesus to reach the entire world, so that people can get to know Jesus, to know the Father and Holy Spirit, but most of all, what the death of Christ and His love for us is truly all about. True wealth lies in knowledge, but this is something the world lost sight of a long time ago. Everyone wants to be wealthy, but true riches can only be found in the knowledge of the Gospel, and those riches are eternal.

Here on earth our riches only last as long as we live, but with our Father in Heaven, we have an everlasting wealth, which is living with our Saviour forever. The Bible is loaded with rich jewels of promises and teachings from both Jesus and all through the inspired writings of the Bible authors, so why do we want to store up treasure here when Jesus says we can store up treasures in Heaven, where thieves can't get to it. (Matt 6:19- 21.) Jen and I have taught our children that we are just passing through this world, leading as many souls to Jesus as we can while doing so.

We concluded our morning prayer by leaving our children safely in God's hands. It was a slow morning; we had not made any plans for that day except to rest. One of the things we had to do, was to go to the Mall to buy a few things for the fridge, yeah right, a few things, married men will understand my meaning. The hand list may be short, but the till slip is long. As a married man I quickly learnt never to argue with the wife, I just could not win.

With my head spinning, what could I say "huh, I love you." It's best to let women be and stay out of their way. Let's face it, asks a man to name his daughter's friends or the birthdays of all his grandchildren, need I continue, he has enough trouble remembering his wives birthday. I think we should move on, we are on thin ice here.

It was my first visit to the new Mall, Hemingways, what a beautiful shopping centre. We took a slow walk through it before going to the food store. Patiently, patiently pushing that trolley; down one isle, up the other isle, patiently, patiently pushing that trolley. Footsore, backache, headache; to top it all, open surgery on my wallet, I was gutted after that. We could not have got home any sooner; I unpacked the groceries then helped Jen put them away. Before anyone could remember my name, I slipped into the room and lay down on the bed for a nap, a well-deserved one at that.

That evening Jen phoned our daughter Sue-Ann, she was glad to hear from her mom.

I was in the lounge watching TV with Jen when she decided to call her. Jen got up and went through to the kitchen to continue her conversation with her, as for me, I decided to leave mom and daughter alone.

A short time later Jen came back with a smile, "Lance could not call us because he ran out of air time and then mislaid his phone. When Sue-Ann phoned him, he heard his phone ring and was able to find it."

With a grin on my face, because I knew what she was thinking "so where was his phone?"

Jen shook her head at me "do you really want to know, it was on his bed under the blankets. It was only because he was in the room when Sue called that he heard it. You guys drive me crazy." She left with a smile, dialling his number.

Jen was happy again, she had spoken to two of the children that day, but the day was not over, later Morgan called, Jen was elated.

Chapter 2

The next morning, while still in bed, Lance called again, Jen sat up to take his call. I listened to talking to him and laughing at whatever it was he said, the conversation took on a serious note for a short time, then they said their goodbyes. Jen turned to me informing me that we would be seeing Lance on the weekend as he has things to do. It was a lovely day, so we decided to go down to the beach for a drive. A quick breakfast and into the car we went.

We drove slowly along the Esplanade until we found a good parking from where we could watch the waves. With the windows open and the fresh sea air in our longs, was blessed moment for me, I took Jens hand, closed my eyes and said a prayer for our children and family, not a lengthy but to the point prayer. It is so important for us to leave our children in the hands of our Father in Heaven. We can't be with them every moment of the day, but their Guardian Angels can, and the Holy Spirit also to guide them in their daily lives. Having done that and having faith that God heard our request, we were able to relax in His promise. (John 14:13.)

Sitting in the car, still holding Jen's hand, watching the waves rolling and crashing against the rocks reminded me of my own life. Some broke down hard on the rocks while others alongside and washed to shore. How many time had I not behaved the same way in life, when thinking I knew best only to discover I did not. Yes there where the few occasions when I was right, but if I had just let God take charge, I would have had more successes than failures.

Our problem is that we want things now, when God has His time, all you have to do is read the story of Abraham and Sarah in the book of Genesis. Even then, God still steps in and straightens out Abrahams' life as he does with ours, what a God we serve.

I watched the seagulls float on pockets of air, hovering patiently over the waters, looking down, waiting for that unsuspecting fish to make a mistake and come to the surface. By watching them, I could not help to think how the devil watches Gods children, waiting for an opportunity to mislead or lure them into his snares. We have to be on our guard every minute of the day, which is why Jen and I pray for each other, our children by name and our family members as well.

A seagull dived into the water and disappeared, seconds later it resurfaced with a small fish in its beak, flicking its head backwards to get the fish to align with their throat, and then gulped it down. Then another seagull dived. I got out of the car to get a better view of the whole scene. Jen joined me and we went and sat on the low wall on the opposite side of the pavement watching the birds in the feeding frenzy which only lasted about two to three minutes, and then it was all over.

The birds floated around for a while, some came down and landed on the rocks some distance away while others flew off in to the distance, my guess was to feed their chicks. There were a few people out taking advantage of the good weather, so we too joined in and went for a stroll, talking to each other while watching a tanker heading into the harbour. I longed to be back home in East London, I said to Jen that I would like for us to retire here, she agreed with me. The rat race of Johannesburg and frustration of the traffic compared to this place was like chalk and cheese. On our way home, to Owen's place, we stopped at the very popular Friesland Dairy for milkshakes, after which we went home.

I went inside to greet Owen, made a cup of tea, sat at the pool while drinking it. I had not yet been to see the old house that I grew up in and wondered how it looked; I had not seen it in years. Sipping my tea, I made the decision to go and have a look, seeing as the town had changed so much, I was curious to see if Moore Street had gone the same way. After washing the mug, yeah, I like to have tea in a mug. I let Jen know I was going to take a drive through the old neighbourhood, she did not mind as she wanted to rest, the sea air and walk had made her sleepy.

Turning off Fleet Street into Curry Street, I slowed the car down, passing some of the flats that friends once lived in, and one that a girlfriend had lived in, further down another block of flats where a good friend I once knew lived. Down the road was where I lived as a child for a while, in a flat. I drove on, in front of me lay Moore Street; I hesitated for a moment, then turned into it and parked the car. The truth being, I felt like a spy, sneaking up on my friends, silly really, they were all long gone from this place.

On both sides of the road lay my childhood, further down on the right stood our old house. The house next door had burnt down some years previously, so I was told, now just a vacant lot collecting junk. Some of the other houses were not too bad, but for the rest, it broke my heart to see them in such poor condition.

I looked about, not a soul to be seen, it made me feel empty inside. This piece of road used to be alive with people, in the morning and after school, we rascals ruled the road.

We played catch, cricket, touch rugby, marbles, tennis, ball and rode our bicycles, all under the watchful eyes of our mothers. Every mother, on both side of the street, was your mother, you did not even think of stepping out of line. Step out of line you face mom, if you were very naughty, dad... not a chance, you do not want to wait for dad to come home and deal with you. There was the odd occasion that we went down to the rocks at the bottom of Moore Street and looked for shells.

I could see all my friends in front of me, their parents leaning on the boundary walls watching us play ball. I saw mom and dad; they too were smiling at us. We were shouting, the girls screaming at us boys for cheating at some or other game we were playing. One of the boys yelled out that we were not cheating; from behind a small girl came and tried to kick him up the jack-o-nory, her legs were to short, so she improvised. She hit him in the front with her small fist, oooh. The man on the moon must have heard us all laughing.

Those were happy days, no worries, no pain, no wars, no loss or sadness. As the picture faded into the mists of time, I emerged to face reality with tears softly flowing down my cheeks. Hastily I looked about; whilst wiping the tears away with the back of my hand; in that momentarily laps of memory, I could not remember where I was. Slowly the brain cells started to lighten up and I remembered. I felt rather silly there for a moment, me a grown man, embarrassed by a few tears, what next!

Once again, before me, an empty street, with buried memories that can only be resurrected by those who once lived here and made them. I waited for the distant sounds of laughter and the loving faces to silently slip away into the portals of the melancholic passages that lead to the sacred memories of my mind, for another day. It may be said of me, that I prefer to be on my own, but not alone.

My mind was a mess; tears flowed freely down my cheeks. What would I not give to be in that spiel again, kicking ball and seeing mom and dad smiling at me. I drove around for who knows how long. The ache in my chest would not ease up. It pained me to know that many of those faces I would not see this side of heaven, life can be so cruel. It lurks in the shadows of our youth and strikes without warning when we reach adulthood; each of us at a different time, and we are totally unprepared for it.

But some were more fortunate than others; their parents had been coaching them financially, which is a big factor in making it in this life. Others had half an idea and few none, to add to that dilemma is education. How we took to education, some of us would rather be out in the open air than bogged down with homework. All these factors play a part in how we handle adulthood, but most of all, how much time do our parents spend on their knees praying for us as we do for our children. There will always be the few who crack under the pressure, and among them will be those who will seek a way out. The majority will always struggle to make ends meet, but how they handle it will depend on their relationship with Christ.

(Matt 11:28) Come to me, all you who labour and are heavy laden and I will give you rest.

Notice that Jesus mentions those that "labour" and are heavy laden. He will give us rest and peace of mind while those that try to make it on their own...well that's their problem, they must work it out, but we can help them to find rest, we can gently introduce them to our Saviour Jesus Christ.

There were those who had parents who encouraged them in their education and were able to help them with their homework.

How I found my way there I do not know, but there I was, parked in front of the Aquarium, down by the beach, neatly tucked into a parking space. I stayed there for a long

time reminiscing over the past, finally I realized
I needed to be near to Jen, I started the car and
drove home.

Chapter 3

Wednesday afternoon was a high day for us. Jen and I returned from the shops to find Lance waiting for us in the lounge, Jen hugged him for a long time, and then I hugged my son. My heart felt so good to see him, to see him looking well, a little thin but then he was tall. Jen was all smiles, but then that was what this holiday was all about, seeing Lance.

He sat on the couch next to his mom while I sat on the opposite side of him in a single soft chair. He made some small talk about work and helping Aubrey (whom Lance had rented a room from for many years) with repairs to trucks. His mood changed and became serious, he started to tell us about his life and all the wrong he had done. Jen placed her hand on his knee and reassured him that we still loved him and that the past was the past. She told him that she had placed him in God's hands a long time before this.

He elaborated on the drugs as well as the drinking that he was involved in and how sorry he was. While telling us his story he kept his gaze from Jen, he never made eye contact with Jen at all. He looked at me when he mentioned that there were people in his life that hurt him and that he had forgiven them. He straightened up and looked me hard in the in the eye and said "Dad, I have forgiven them." There was a long silence as he held my gaze, then I understood. "Okay Lance, I hear you." Our eyes still locked on, I nodded my head. He looked down again saying how good he felt after he had forgiven them and that he had never felt such peace before.

We continued with small talk about Heavenly things. Jen shared some moments of her life where she too had to forgive her transgressors. As for me, I found it difficult to forgive, had it not been for Jen's patience in teaching me to say sorry and mean it, I don't think I would be a Christian today. She pointed out the connection of being sorry and honest, that they are one. To say sorry is to say I did it; to say I did it is to be honest; to be honest is to please Jesus by keeping the ninth commandment (Rev. 14:12). Jen is still working with me on forgiving, she is winning, and that is because the Holy Spirit is on her side, and both are helping me to overcome this weakness of character.

It was time for him to leave us and return home. We walked him to his bakkie which he and Aubrey had rebuilt for the use of the small company Aubrey had. They had done a fantastic job repairing it. Lance did the spray painting which was perfect, it looked like a new pickup, we made no short work of letting him know how proud we were of his work.

They needed the vehicle for transporting parts to and from the workshop. We could see that Lance appreciated our praise of his work. He was smiling from ear to ear. He got in behind the steering wheel and started the engine; it hummed like a new one. They had truly done a great job all round, now they no longer had to rely on anyone else to collect or deliver parts for them. We said our goodbyes and off he drove in their new bakkie with Jen and I waving to him but he never looked back.

We waited until he turned the corner before going back inside the house. I could not get those words out of my mind that he had never felt such peace before. It reminded me of the children of Abraham during the time of the plagues. Then it dawned on me, it is only the children of the Lord who find peace in the midst of a storm.

(Exodus 9:24) so there was hail, and fire mingled with the hail, very grievous,   such as there was none like it in all the land of Egypt since it became a nation.

(Exodus 9:26) Only in the land of Goshen, where the children of Israel were, was there no hail.

Think about it for a moment, Goshen, a place that the Egyptians regarded as place so far beneath them that they would not put foot there, but our GOD, our GOD who created all beings and animals and nature went there to protect the Israelites, He goes anywhere to fetch and protect HIS children and to give them peace. Never stop praying for our children and their families.

(John 14:27) Peace I leave with you, my peace I give unto you: Let not your hearts be troubled, neither let it be afraid.

From a small child, Jen had taught Lance the ways of our Father in Heaven. He would come to understand the peace he felt, he wanted peace and he found it:

(Luke 11: 9) And I say unto you, Ask, and it shall be given you, seek, and ye shall find; knock, and it shall be opened unto you.

(1 John 5:14) "And this is the confidence that we have in Him, that, if we ask anything according to His will, he heareth us:" Lance also knew that every promise had a condition, and that is we who have to show Jesus that we are on His side. How do we do that? Well we do it by doing as He asks us to do, and that is to:

(1 John 3:22) And whatsoever we ask, we receive of him, because we keep his

commandments, and do those things that are pleasing in his sight.

Chapter 4

Thursday morning was no different to any other day as far as our holiday was concerned. The sun was shining; there was a gentle breeze and few clouds in the sky, a perfect day for swimming, if you were into that sort of thing. Jen was in the kitchen while I sat outside enjoying the morning air, when I heard Jen's cell phone ring, it was Lance. Jen came out to me and with a quirky smile said "he wants only to speak to dad."

Taking the phone from her I politely pulled a tongue at her "Hi Lance, what's up?"

"Hey, dad, what a lovely morning! I'm looking out over a field thinking of ouma (granny). Do you remember her favourite hymn?

"Hey Lance, yes it is a lovely morning. Ouma has been gone for many years, I think it was..." he cut me short.

"It was 'I Come to the Garden Alone', remember it now?"

I was smiling, he was not quite the teenager when she died yet he remembered. "Yes, now I do."

"Shame dad, how could you forget? I'm sitting here singing it and it is so...so just right.

The morning mood with the bird and plants make it so real."

There was a pause, then "Now I know why she loved that song. You once told me she grew up on a farm. Hey man, it all comes together, yeah, she saw the beauty in that song. She saw what other people could not see but the words."

"I think it gave her peace to sing that hymn, it took her back to a time of blissful comfort to when she was a child."

"Hey dad, that was grandmas' spot in her head, where she could escape to and pray. It was her secret garden, hers and Jesus', I like that idea, a place of tranquillity."

"She had to have it Lance! I replied, she had a hard life growing up poor. We all need a secret place in our heads to escape to in order to stay sane; it's that or the loony bin. So many people don't realize that they need to take time out of life. Take a walk by yourself, go to a library, sit in a corner and read a book from the children section, one that will make you smile. Do something by yourself, sit in a park and enjoy the sunshine while in that secret place you have created in your mind that only you know of. Lance it is important to chill out every few days for half an hour or so, we really need it."

"Hey dad, you sound like Bob Marley without the joint." Then Lance began to laugh. I could just imagine his thoughts at that moment, his straight-laced dad sucking on a foot long reefer, a head of dreadlocks shrouded in a cloud of dragon breath bopping around reggae music.

I started to laugh at the thought "I like some of his music Lance." Lance came right in and serious.

"Hey dad, it's hard to focus when the world is going mad. I have my spot but sometimes I can't get in, so I pray out loud and I don't care what people think of me, I speak to God when I want to, I have to keep in touch with Jesus dad, if I don't I will lose out on my salvation."

My heart soared like an eagle into the blue sky above me to hear these words from my son whom I was so worried about. I prayed so much for him as did his mother. He had problem, we all have problem, our children have problem and we know of them. Jen and I have always tried to help our children and because of that, they have been open with us. It hurt deeply to hear some of the things that they were involved in, which only intensified of prayers for them.

'Dad, do you have a spot that you go to?"

It took a moment for me to realize that Lance had asked me a question "Yes Lance I do, I go there often and I know what you mean when you say that sometimes it is hard to focus. Then I have days when I just do not want to come back from it, it's so peaceful."

"Hey man, dad, I know exactly what you mean, I have the same thoughts. Hey dad, don't tell mom, or she will want photos of the place. Remember when you guys came down one year and mom took photos of us. We even tried to hide from her because every time she saw us, she took shots of us."

We laughed at that, it was crazy then, but looking back, we could see the funny side of it. "Yes I remember, it was as if that camera was part of her face." We keep those photos in an album now along with other happy holiday snaps. There was a silence as we reminisced.

When he spoke again, his voice was different, sombre and distant "Dad...dad...there were people in my life...people who hurt me. I want you to know that I have forgiven them...dad...did you hear me?"

"Yes I heard you." The tone of my response was not what he wanted to hear, I sort of brushed it aside as if a thing that was part of life.

His response to my reply was punitive "Dad, I said I forgave them."

For a moment there I felt an enigmatical amusement overcome me as Lance had never before used that tone of voice on me before. Then it dawned on me, that my son was asking me, or more like it, ordering me to exercise forbearance towards his wrong doers should I ever find out who they were. I decided to ask him who hurt him and how. "Okay Lance, I hear you, no action from me…"

"Do you give me your word dad?" he asked before I could finish my sentence.

Now all the red flags went up. I wanted to know what had happened to my son, and by whom. "Lance, what happened and who did it, I want to know?" my voice became stern.

He raised his voice a little "Dad, you're not listening to me, it's over. I have forgiven them, it is in the past and I have peace and I want your word that you will not retaliate. I know what you can be like when someone tries hurts us, so please dad, swear to me you will let it go. Swear to me you will forgive and forget, put it behind you, please dad."

I thought for a while what could have happened to him, my mind was racing too fast to settle on any one factor. "How can I forgive if

I do not know what I am supposed to forgive?" my temper was rising, anger about to settle in, but I was speaking to my son, so I managed to calm myself.

"Dad, it's called trust, trust in me, can you do that?"

"You know I trust you Lance, okay," I paused. " because my son Lance has asked me to forgive persons unknown to me for harming him, harm I know not of my Saviour, I forgive these people, I will do my best to control myself should I find out the extent of the harm. " Then I remembered he asked me not to retaliate. "I will not take revenge against them."

His voice descended into a calm peaceful tone "Thanks dad. I know it's hard for you, but you need to come to that garden and find peace, just like ouma and me. Hey think of all the trees that are there that aren't here on earth and the plants that are in Heavens garden. Man, the animals, man, truly out of this world. Dad if anything should happen to me before mom dies"

I cut him short, this conversation was about to turn melancholic, "Lance, you are not going to die before mom. You are young and strong, and years still lay before you so stop it."

"I know dad, but you know I drive those huge trucks and abnormal machines, anything can happen on those mountain passes."

I capitulated to his reasoning. My brother had an unfortunate accident on a wet mountain road which left my sister-in-law in a wheelchair. Lance was one of a few chaps that could drive those monster machines. "Lance you know full-well that mom and I pray for you every day for your safety, we can only ask God to watch over you for us." Lance, like so many of our young people loved his beer, he more than others. Often we feared for his safety and were brought down hard on to our knees asking God to take charge of his life, to send the Holy Spirit in and speak to him. I was taken aback by what he asked me to do next.

His voice was soft, calm and steady "Dad, if anything should happen, this is what I want you to do with my body." He spoke clearly and to the point, he knew exactly what he wanted done. This was not a spur of the moment decision; the way he laid it all out to me, assure me of this. Having been a teacher for fourteen years, showed me he had spent much time thinking this through thoroughly and carefully planning of each aspect so as not to hurt any member of the family. He concluded with "Dad, this must remain between us, please, until that day."

I had listened very carefully to every word he said, this was not just some chit chat between father and son, this was a very important discussion, a testament, it had to be taken seriously and remembered. "Lance you have my word, it will be as you asked. Can I tell you what I want done?"

I shared with him how I would go to the beach and watch the waves as a child when my father came home tipsy, and began to talk nonsense to the neighbours, or when he brought home his drunken friends and he wanted my sister and me to make music for them. A drunk person can't appreciate music, so I went down to the sea and the waves, down to the rocks and spoke to Jesus there and asked him to help my father come to his senses. This went on for many years, so for many years on a Saturday afternoon I went down to the rock, sea and waves to speak to my Saviour. "Lance, when I pass away, cremate my body and place me in a place where the family can come and pay their respects if they wish. Then after two or three years, inter me in the sea. Will you see to that?"

"Hey dad, that's real cool, yeah, I will do that for you. I never knew oupa drank?"

"Yes he did Lance, Jesus answered ouma's and my prayers before she died. He stopped drinking before she died. She loved Jesus all her life and I truly believe he did that for her because of that."

"Does Morgan know about your wish?"

"No, you call him and talk to him; he would love a surprise call from you."

"Yeah…I will. Yeah, dad, cool…in the sea, neat. Dad I must go…I love you dad."

"Hey I love you too Lance, see you on Sabbath."

"Yeah dad…on Sabbath."

He hung up leaving me with a mind swirling with new thoughts. It's strange how a phone call can change the mood of one's mind. Here I was enjoying the morning air and sun, now that pleasure is forgotten and replaced by thoughts of the discussion I have just had with my son. I realized that I had better see to it that all my insurances are up to date.

Chapter 5

Over the past few years I have watched a number of movies about Vietnam, all of which depicted the Vietcong taking a beating when in reality that was not always the case. One night I decided to go and watch one of these movies and was quite moved by what I saw. The director had focused his attention on the compassion the military showed to its soldier's loved ones after they fell in battle. The plot did not work out so well as they expected it would with the audience.

The camera was placed on the dashboard of the car as it entered the military housing compound, driving slowly around; looking for the address they were to deliver the sad news to. I watched as children stopped their play and mothers gathered them inside, praying for the two officers to drive past. It reminded me of a little white ball on a roulette wheel, all eyes fixed on it, but in this case praying for it not to pop into your number socket.

Finally it would stop in front of a house and the camera would focus on the wife at the door. One could not hear her words but clearly make them out "no, no, you have the wrong house, no, you are mistaken, not my Bobby." But sadly it was. The two officers would slowly leave whilst neighbours came running to give her moral support and comfort.

As time went by they made more recent movies of the US soldiers in other battles and as it would happen, I saw how times had changed. The two officers were replaced by a taxi driver who nervously entered the living compound with a telegram to be met by the same look of fear from the women and older children. My respect for the US military abruptly vanished. Why the change? Who forgot that the man who fell actually gave his life for a politicians cause? We do not go to war because we like it, we get drafted into the military service and have no say in the matter.

When I did my bit on the border, I did not want to know how my wife would be told nor my parents. Having them worry every time a car pulled up in front of the house or a strange looking letter arrive in the post scaring the life out of them was not what I wanted. If I was to be killed, then so be it, but by the grace of God, I was not.

But this day there was not black car with two officers or a taxi with a telegram in his hand. This morning at about eight my phone rang, it was my daughter Sue-Ann and she was hysterical. I could hear her shouting before I got the phone to my ear "My brother is dead, Lance is dead, dad Lance hung himself this morning. My brother is dead."

Time stood still. My mouth dried up. I broke out in a cold sweat. A slight dizziness came over me. A voice called out in my head "Hold on, hold on" I fought back the shock I was experiencing. "Sue, calm down, where is Lance?"

She just managed to tell me that he was at Aubrey's house. To this day I do not remember the rest of that conversation. Jen came into the room and wanted to know what the commotion was all about. I sat her down and as calmly as I possibly could, I said to her "Lance is no longer with us."

Her face paled "What are you saying to me?"

I looked at my wife and saw her age right before my eyes as I said "Lance passed away this morning."

She began to cry "That's not possible, what really happened?"

That's when I felt my chest tear open and my heart bled for the second time in my life. The first time was when my father died in my arms in the hospital and he kept his eyes on me as the heart attack took him from us.

"Jen...Jen...Lance hung himself this morning." Jens world collapsed.

All that morning is a blur, to try and make up something just to fill in that morning would not do justice to my family. My life picks up again when we later that afternoon went out to visit Aubrey and his sister Doreen at their house. The police and the coroner had already been and taken Lance away. Aubrey, who had not touched a drink in many, many years, was holding onto a class of brandy, I could not blame him, seeing as he was the one who found Lance. He sat there, deep in his own thoughts, every now and then shaking his head, then taking a sip of his drink. He looked at me; it was then that I noticed that there was something missing from his soul. Previous visits were a joy, he was cheerful and bright, his eyes shone, today that was all gone.

During my life I have seen bodies of men who had died only minutes before I arrived on the scene. They still had colour in their faces, but the life was missing from their eyes. Aubrey reminded me of them that day when I saw his eyes.

Sipping from the glass in his hand, he looked once more at me "Come" was all he said and got up. I followed him. He led me outside and began to show me some of the plants in his yard. We moved closer to his workshop and around to the opposite side of the trucks he was working on. Slowly he took me to the entrance of the work shop and said "this is where he did it."

I looked around and proceeded to walk into the area. On the work bench were neatly rolled up strong cords, about three of them. A bakkie was parked in the shop in reverse but not all the way in. I looked at Aubrey and he pointed to a beam above me.

"He put that red rope over that beam and climbed up using that step ladder over there." The stepladder had been moved from leaning against the beam over to the tree some meters away. "Those ropes weren't there last night that was done this morning. Doreen saw him sitting on the back wall watching the sunrise. He put the dogs away so that they would not have to see him, he loved animals." Aubrey stopped talking.

I picked up the rope from the workshop floor and held it for a good while, the placed it in the back of the bakkie. For some time I looked up at where my son took his life, then I knew what he was doing on that wall this morning, he was talking to God as he always did. He was telling God of his plan and why.

Back in the house Aubrey told us that he used to say that one day he was going to do it, he was just looking for the right tree. He chose a wooden beam in the back corner of a workshop to end it all.

Thoughts began to flow through my mind like an endless river carrying anger and vengeance with it. Who drove my son to this, what did they do to him and why? My thoughts were interrupted, Doreen had made tea, I was going to have vengeance. With my mind made up, I was able to enjoy my tea.

This is a late entry into my book. Aubrey died of a broken heart about a year later. Due to some devious manipulating circumstances, we were prohibited from attending his funeral.

We will never forget Aubrey Schwartz for his kindness to our son Land Richard Hillier; he was a second father to him. Aubrey filled the gap I could not, being so far away, what a friend he was to all who knew him. His sister came to live with him after his illness to take care of him and Lance, Doreen soon learned to love Lance as a son and treated him as her own.

I met Aubrey when I was but a boy back in the day; he was a strikingly handsome young lad making eyes at my cousins. I had five girl cousins that the fellows used to come and visit. He had a head of serious black hair which with age turned a pepper grey. Doreen now looks after his business of repairing trucks.

Both my wife and I prayed for Aubrey and Doreen, now we pray for Doreen that our Father in heaven will watch over her and give her comfort and strengthen her each day.

Chapter 6

Our daughter had arrived; Morgan could only get a flight on Sunday. Evening came so quickly with my mind being so occupied that I almost forgot that we had to fetch Morgan. Jen reminded me that it was almost time for the plane to arrive. We headed for the airport only to be told when arriving there that the plane had not left Johannesburg due to heavy rains. It was about five hours later that Morgan and the other passengers arrived at the East London airport. Torrential rains almost cancelled the flight completely; fortunately it cleared up enough for all the delayed flights to take off safely.

Our concern about whom we were to get to do the burial preparations, were soon put to rest. Fortunately, a friend of Owens gave him a name of a trustworthy funeral parlour in East London from whom we were able to get good advice on which steps to follow. This allowed us to progress smoothly with our part of the proceedings of the funeral.

Our first priority was to identify Lance at the police mortuary and sign the release papers to have him taken to the parlour, this we did on Monday morning.

All I could think about is who I could call upon to do the service. Sue knew of a pastor.

After making contact with him he told her that he was already booked up for days. I wanted someone who would do justice to the memory of Lance and seeing that this person did not know Lance, well, it did not sit right with me. I continued to pray about the matter asking my friend Jesus to help me in finding the right person, all that day I kept my mind on my Saviour, asking for the right person to come to mind.

The next morning we got in touch with Denzel at Integrity Funerals to find out if they had received Lance. We were told that the coroner had not yet completed his autopsy, once that was done we would be notified for a viewing. Then later that morning we received a call from Denzel saying that we could view Lance in two days' time, because he was so tall, they had to have an extra-long coffin made for him, which meant that the service would take place a day later than first thought. Yet still in my mind was this worry of whom could I call on to do the service. It was prearranged that Lance would be cremated; only I knew what was to happen to his remains.

Finally we were able to view Lance. I went in first with Denzel to make sure all was in order. I was truly pleased at how the parlour beauticians had taken care of Lance's make-over, now my family could come in and pay their last respects. The marks on his neck were well concealed and his jaw reset. He looked as if he had died in his sleep, a touch of compassion I would not forget from a stranger I had never met before.

Later in his office I noticed a well-crafted wooden box and asked him about it.

Denzel reached over to it and moved it towards me. "This is a sample of what we offer to our clients for the deceased. We place their ashes in it, it helps with closure. The loved ones can keep it, or inter it when they are ready."

It was really a neat piece of wood-work; I ordered one for Lance's ashes. We spoke for a while, while my family readied themselves to leave. All the way home my mind was on the service the next day. Again I called on the only one I could whom I knew would save the day, Jesus. I prayed all the way back to Owens house.

Arriving at his house I sat on the veranda praying that this problem would soon be resolved. I had lost all sense of time; next thing I knew, I was being call in for lunch and still I had not received a solution to my dilemma. If my memory serves me correctly, we ate in silence that afternoon.

Feeling better having had lunch, I went back outside and sat on the veranda. It was then that my Saviour answered my prayers. An illustration came into my mind, an illustration that could only have come from a divine source, I had never thought of anything like that in my life before. I went inside to find pen and paper, moments later I was writing down thoughts as they came into my mind from the Holy Spirit.

The most amazing thing happened to me that afternoon; I felt the presence of the Holy Spirit with me as I wrote down those thoughts. It all fell into place and made complete sense. But most of all, it did what I wanted it to do, it did justice to the memory Lance. I closed my eyes and gave thanks and glory to my Father in Heaven. I never expected that He would choose me to do the service. I read through it, folded the sheets of paper up and went inside to announce that I would be doing the service for my son.

Now I prayed for strength to carry it through without breaking down, I knew my Jesus would send the Holy Spirit to strengthen me and my Guardian Angel to uphold me during the service, but I had to call on my Father and my Saviour, for without them I am a thing of naught.

I prayed and read Isaiah 41: 10-13; 10 Fear thou not; for I am with thee: be not dismayed; for I am thy God: I will strengthen thee; yea, I will help thee; yea, I will uphold thee with the right hand of my righteousness.

11 Behold, all they that were incensed against thee shall be ashamed and confounded: they shall be as nothing; and they that strive with thee shall perish.

12 Thou shalt seek them, and shalt not find them, even them that contended with thee: they that war against thee shall be as nothing, and as a thing of nought.

13 For I the LORD thy God will hold thy right hand, saying unto thee, Fear not; I will help thee.

As always, I claimed the promise it for my strength and for the strength of my family. Should Satan try to intervene and cause me to break down and disrupt the service, he had to be bound and held down while my Saviour was being lifted up before the people in that chapel who would come to say good-bye to Lance. Nothing at all would be permitted to disrupt that service, therefore I claimed that promise. It was not I who thought up those words, I only penned the words and would repeat them to those who would be in the chapel. The words the Holy Spirit gave me were meant to bring comfort to my family, and to those who loved Lance and may have lost a family member in such a way as we lost Lance.

My mind was at rest, my heart was beating quietly, I could now give comfort to my family. Jesus did not promise that we would not suffer pain and loss on this earth, but he did promise eternal life if we followed Him.

Chapter 7

We arrived at the Chapel a little ahead of time to check that all the preparations were done, I checked the microphone, yes it worked. At the door stood a well-dressed man in a dark suit, ready to hand out... It's not easy recalling those moments, I still feel the pain, I guess I will still feel the pain when lying on my own death bed thinking of those I loved and laid to rest.

The time came for me to get up and deliver the message. Before going up, I closed my eyes and asked my friend to be with me, He answered right away, "Fear thou not." I stood up and took my place behind the podium. Looking at each person there, making eye contact with each one individually. I felt a warm strength surround me, and I knew I was in safe hands.

Calmly I greeted them: "Good afternoon. Thank you all for coming to pay your respects to Lance. I am not one who likes to sermonize; I find a story far better to remember than a sermon. It may be strange for you to come to a funeral service and be told a story. As we proceed I am sure you will all understand why I chose this method."

(I turned to take a look at the casket behind me in which my son lay. Turning my attention back to family and friends I began with the story that the Holy Spirit had given me.)

Two women, living in the same town, both pregnant, oblivious of each other, are taken to the same hospital on the same day upon which both deliver a healthy baby boy. All goes well for the babies and their mothers and soon they are discharged from the hospital. Totally unaware that their boys would one day leave this earth in the same manner, they pass each other in the lobby of the hospital.

Both boys grow up in normal middle class families; both enjoy a happy life with their siblings. Then comes the day they have to start school, this is where we divide the story; we will be following one boy whom we will call the first boy.

The first boy is an average student of average intelligence, battles with languages, but loves sport, yet manages to get by even though his grades are nothing to shout about. He meets up with new friends, and as young boys do, they try things out. Soon they are into drugs and alcohol and his grades start dropping even lower.

Desperately his parents try to encourage him to leave his friends and press on, but to no avail, he leaves school and finds a job.

The years pass, he his drinking more, taking stronger drugs and working less. He just cannot hold onto a job. He soon realized that there is no hope left for him, his life is like a roller-coaster ride, up and down and out of control. He begins to wonder who is in charge of his life, why is it always going wrong. One day he decides to take charge and straighten out his life, but where to start. His parent never taught him about life, they never gave him any guide lines to follow in case of an emergency like now. He gave up trying to walk the straight and narrow path everyone spoke of; to him those were just words, nothing else, just words.

Searching deep into his soul he found nothing to cling to, just emptiness. He succumbed to the one true realization about his life, it is too late, the roller-coaster of his life was way out of control and that his life was a complete mess. In his subconscious mind he tries to head up to the front of the roller-coaster and see who is steering him through all this chaos. Coach by coach; year by year searching for the driver. Many times he saw how he fell from the roller-coaster and tried desperately to hang on. He wept that there was nobody there to help him. So many times he fell out of the roller-coaster, so many times he saw how it became more and more difficult to get back onto the roller-coaster.

Despondent, lonely and feeling fear mingled with anger, he decided to bite the bullet and press on. Sailing through his memories he would stop, and pause, for a moment. He remembered a young girl inviting him to a church youth camp. He thinks to himself and asks himself where he would have been now had he gone and had fought against peer pressure from his friends.

Finally he reaches the leading coach, alas; there was no one at the wheel. The young man takes hold of the break-lever and pauses for a moment; he knows that if he pulls the lever his life will end. Why not he thinks, my life is on a downhill spiral and I can't do a thing about it. He pulls in the lever, the roller-coaster of life stops...it's over".

(I waited a few seconds before I I started on the second boy. Again I looked at each person in that small chapel that afternoon; all eyes were fixed on me. It's difficult to explain, but I could see that each person was in a special place of their own. I looked down at my notes and began.)

The second boy had very much the same life, but there was a significant difference. From an early age his mother taught him about Jesus and how Jesus helped people here on earth, when He was here. The boy's parents had bought a set of Bible Stories Books and read them to their children at evening worship. They loved the stories. They also taught their children to pray before going to bed at night. They got to choose a verse from the Bible before kneeling beside their beds. These verses were chosen to strengthen their characters. And when money was tight or when decisions were to be made, prayers were offered up for guidance.

When prayers were answered, they would call the family together and tell them, they would then kneel down and give thanks to God for His mercies and kindness. So the second boy grew up seeing how God answered prayers, not only in his family's life, but in his own life as well.

When he too came to the point where life was too much for him, when drinking and past drug abuse had taken its toll on him, he too headed up to the front of the roller-coaster of life. On his way up, traveling through his thoughts he saw how many times he was thrown off, only to be saved by the hands he knew so well that pulled back on again. The hands he had seen in the pictures in those books his mother had read to him as a child.

Finally he reached the front coach, and there he saw the driver, a man with snow white hair and pierced hands, and the same hands that saved him so many times before. He had both hands on the wheel, carefully steering the young man's life through all its difficulties and troubles. The young man recognized the driver instantly for he had known Him all his life, they had had many conversations together, when things were not going so well and when life was good, always sharing the day and thoughts with his friend and Saviour.

He came up alongside his Saviour and sat down next to Him. He placed his hand on His hand and said I cannot go on, life has become too much for me. You have done all you can for me, but I messed up, not you, please forgive me. If I continue on this path, I will lose my salvation; I do not want to lose you, please give me the strength to do this, rather than lose my salvation.

Jesus put his arm around the young man's shoulder and drew him closer to himself and in a quiet voice said, I know your concern, because you always called me when you needed me, or just to talk and I have always loved our conversations, today I understand. What I appreciated most about you, is that you would talk to me about your life even when you were fine, I liked that. Because you wanted me around I stayed close to you and helped you every time you called on me. I had a friend like you many years ago. He too went astray but never forgot me and when he asked me for strength to topple two mighty supporting columns, I gave it to him. He died that day, I will call him one day, I have not forgotten him. I had his name recorded in My Holy Word."

The young man slowly reached out and took hold of the break lever as Jesus put His arm around his shoulder and drew him close to Himself. With His other hand Jesus touched the young man's hand that rested on the lever, giving him assurance, and slowly the young man pulled back, his roller-coaster of life eased to a halt.

I looked at the congregation, nobody stirred, they were waiting for something, as if they knew there was more to come, and there was more to this parable.

Now the time of the end has come and the world as we know it is over. Jesus is welcoming His saints into heaven, and there is our second young man walking up to Jesus, he is a little, surprised because he did not believe he had found enough grace in the eyes of the LORD. Jesus welcomes him and smiles and calls him by name. They hug, he kisses Jesus on the neck, then Jesus directs his attention to a large man in the distance, a man with long, long hair. Young man, I believe that both you and Samson have something in common, go over to him, I told him about you a short while ago, he is expecting you.

I saw the surprise in their eyes when I mentioned Samson, yes, we all have forgotten Samson. Hebrews 11:32 the Faith chapter mentions Samson, God had not forgotten Samson. I ended with these words "Never be so quick to condemn those who take their own lives, that truth alone, lies with our Saviour Jesus Christ.

My daughter then came up and read messages sent in by friends. After that a friend of Lance's, one of his ex-bosses told us of a trip they took up into the mountains to do some work up there for the Baptist Church. He turned to Jen and looked at her and told her that Lance had rededicated his life to God that day and they saw the change in him. I grabbed hold of the podium, I knew that if I did not, I would lose it, Jen wept.

We closed with an appropriate hymn 'I come to the garden alone'. During the hymn I had to press the button to lower the casket, I found the button but could not bring myself to press it, as we drew closer to the end of the hymn; I barely managed to press it.

After the service we went home, Morgan drove the car. Arriving at home I went and lay down, I was emotionally drained, Jen came and sat with me. Three days later we collected Lance's ashes, they were in a well-made light wooden box that I had paid for in advance. As a family, we decided that Morgan and I would go back home by car and Jen would follow in a few days by bus.

<u>Part 3</u>

A Journey of Healing

Chapter 8

Both Morgan and I began work the day after arriving back in Johannesburg. It had been a long and quiet journey home. My heart went out to my wife and family, they were going to miss Lance's calls. He would call me every week or so just to unwind his frustrations; sometimes we would chat about the state of the world, other times we had serious talks about the family and the problems within. These concerned him very much, as in many families, we too did not all see eye-to-eye.

Our two boys, Lance and Morgan, two completely different characters, yet they understood and loved each other very much. They had shared some great times together leaving Morgan with some good memories. I had to be strong and not forget that I still had my living family to take care of while inwardly grieving for my absent Lance. Nowhere in life's book is there a chapter of how to balance loss and life, it just does not fit in. I had to be the catalyst that holds them all together as best I could, is that not what a father is supposed to do?

The first few days back at work I was finding it difficult to focus on my tasks, I kept expecting Lance to call, the call never came. Life at work became so surreal that it was almost mundane. As much as I threw myself into my work, I literally got lost in it. I began to make such simple silly mistakes. Finally I downed pens and went for a long walk around the campus, while reconstructing my thoughts. I spotted a bench beneath a tree and took refuge there, a time to think, a long while to weep for my loss, something I could not do at home.

Jen was back at home now, and a few weeks later, I'm not sure how many later, she asked me to take her to see her psychiatrist for a visit. Her words made no sense to me, my mind was every which way but up. One thing I did know, there was a battle taking place in my brain, a war had started and I was losing it.

When Jen was called into his office, I went in with her. The doctor spoke to her and asked her a few questions, then turned to me. If my memory serves me correctly, he asked me two questions, and then I broke down. My head began to hurt, well, it was in constant pain since I found out how the reason my son had taken to drugs and alcohol, to forget the hurt and painful memories.

I wanted to face those people and do damage to them, but I kept remembering my promise to Lance, my mind was a mess, I could not think straight, but I do remember asking him for help. Mingled in all this mess was an anger that I had never before experienced toward those who hurt my son. I still had a spot of good sense to know that without help, my whole family could be affected by any action I might take. Two days later I was admitted into a clinic in Randburg that caters for depression, stress and who knows what else. Say what you like, call me by any name you want, I was a certified nut case and I did not and still do not mind being called that, big deal. There are so many of us walking the streets who think we are fine, when we are not.

Morgan took me to the clinic and I checked in at around lunch time. After all the formalities, I was taken to my room, a double room, it was empty, and so I chose the bed next to the window. From there I could look down onto the clinic grounds and across over to Sandton. The first thing I did was to close my door and have a prayer; I placed my family firmly in God's hands and prayed for their health and safe keeping. I then followed up with placing my health in His hands and asking for help to recover at His pace.

I took a stroll around the building before going through to dinner. The dining room was divided into three sections, youth, addicts, and the depressed; neither group was allowed to talk to the other group, yeah sure. The addicts and youth groups were almost the same size, small while we dominated the scene. I chose a table at the rear of my group against the wall; I was alone there and had a good view of my inmates. I have always had a love to study people's walk, facial expressions and how they like to dress. As a young boy I could tell who was walking into our house by their footsteps before we saw them. I could tell when family members were telling lies by their expressions on their faces and so on. All I wanted to do now was to see how people changed as they improved.

Monday morning I got up early and took a shower, went down for breakfast and decided to find out what to do. The weekly programs had not arrived, so I took to the grounds enjoying the sun and fresh air. I began to wonder how my appointments would be arranged for me to see my psychiatrist, I was politely shown the notice board and where the weekly programs could be found, they had arrived. Fortunately for me, I only had to see my shrink the next day at five in the afternoon. Even though I now had a program, I stayed out of it all but checked the events for the next day. All the while my head hurt, though I was able to think a little more clearly. Off to the medication station I went with my aching head, there I was given two pills and a glass of water, the medication did nothing for me at all. I wanted to leave the clinic and go over to the chemist, to get something stronger.

"Do you have a gate pass from you Doctor" asked the gate keeper.

I learned that after the first week, with your Doctors permission, you may get a day pass, my head hurt, so I went and lay on my bed, soon I was asleep. When I woke up, I felt a lot better, and very hungry, providentially dinner was soon to be served.

I took my place in the dining room, the youth were behind me, the addicts were on a raised level to my left and the rest of us took the main part of the dining room. The youth were rather loud and one could not help overhearing their complaints. It became quite clear that some of them had major parent issues. They complained about the parents not seeing them or giving them a voice. Others protested of not having quality time with their parents, but they would rather run off to be with their friends to social clubs, and being the town's socialites.

I felt the anger rise within my soul, accompanied by hostile thoughts toward their parents. My head began to hurt again and I knew I had to get out of there. Many young people would change their attitudes and love their parents if their parents would take time to listen to their children and spend some quality time with them. All we have to do is open our eyes and we will see how parents are trying to impress their friends, rather impress your children.

It made me think of the Apostle Paul, a learned man, poor, a tent maker yet working with his hands to feed himself and those in need, when brought before the Roman leaders and King Agrippa, he was poorly dressed and dirty, yet he spoke eloquently, quietly and calmly, which impressed the king. Do we speak quietly, calmly and eloquently to our children? Do we?

Who was it that washed Christ's feet with tears and dried them with her hair? An outcast, a redeemed prostitute, and her name was Mary. Redeemed because Jesus listened to her and did not judge her but forgave her in a quiet loving voice, she responded to his call. All our children want is for us to listen to them, for us to hear their side of the story, and hug them every day and not to forget to let them know how much they are loved; then we will begin to hear of less suicides. One of my friends had shot himself, his father had never given him the time of day. I have a few more stories like his, how many do you have?

Not all suicides are a result of parental misconduct. There are many reasons why young people take their own lives, some we will never know why, some because of illness...so many reasons. As parents, let us start with our children whom we can help. We may not be able to prevent the act from taking place, but we can give them a Heavenly chance, as was Samson, found in the Book of Judges.

We start by introducing them to our Savour Jesus Christ. First we pray for them and ask God to prepare their minds to meet your proposal. After a few days, approach them but pray before you talk to them ; pray every time before you talk to them and do not get upset if they turn away in the beginning, keep praying and quietly approach them. Remember you have asked the one person who helped you and me at some point in our lives to help them now, so think how it went for you when God helped you. A slow introduction; morning worship, Grace before meals and evening worship. Make a start to save a life, start with your own. To help a smoker give up smoking, you must first have been a smoker. Helping the lost you must have been lost at one time.

This is a parable: A young man along life's path trips and falls into a financial gorge, a very deep gorge. He can't see his way out and feels helpless. He calls on God for help.

The first person to pass by is a stranger who hears his call for help. The stranger promises to go and find help, but never returns.

The second is a group of his friends, but they are having a social day and say they will call back later, they never do.

The third one is a man of the cloth and all he can offer is a prayer.

Then a fourth person to come by and hears someone calling for help. He calls to the trapped man and tells him to move out of the way, he is coming down, and so slides down the side of the gorge to where the man is. The trapped man is furious at him for doing what he just did as they are now both trapped. "No" says the man, "not so, I have been down here before and I know the way out, follow my instructions and you will be out of this gorge soon." And I promise to stay with you until your problem is resolved. And so God answered his prayer by sending someone who could really help him.

When you and I were lost, was it not Jesus to whom we turned, and was it not Him who heard our cry, was it not Him who came down to save us and gently brought us back to the light?

Chapter 9

Tuesday morning, was a cloudy day, but my heart was filled with a bright shiny new goal in life, step one – get well, as well as I can get, with all that has happened to me. I had done about three years of body building some years before, coupled with much reading on mind readiness. Therefore I knew about positive thinking and mind preparedness, today was day one of wellness. After showering, I checked the program, okay so it's all about stigma, should be interesting.

I don't remember all the lessons as they were presented to us word for word; you must understand I was not myself back then. I had to do research and rely on memory to help me record all the classes; I do have the lists of classes as they were laid out day by day for the three weeks that I was there. I must add that my research has provided me with more than what my memory has.

Entering the room, I saw that the chairs were set in a semi-circle and three rows deep, not a bad idea. Many of the patients were already seated and soon after the speaker arrived and introduced himself as Doctor. I liked him immediately, his whole approach to the class was so down to earth, I could see from sitting in the back row how everybody's attitude became so relaxed. He wrote one word on the white board – STIGMA.

In short, the word stigma, translated into easy terms simply means ignominy, shame, humiliation or dishonour. It's shameful that in some areas of society, symptoms of psychopathology as a treatment make people feel uncomfortable around those who are being treated for 'abnormal' behaviour. Much of society today does not take the time to read or try and find out about the next persons problem. It's just too much effort, so they remain uneducated in these matters and rather choose to brand the people who have 'abnormal 'behaviour. I find that sort of approach so demeaning, irresponsible and a lack of intelligence.

If we could but only understand that intelligence promotes our intellectual status and alleviates poverty which in turn promotes good health, which assuages suicides, and that is what this is all about.

What is mental health stigma? It can be divided into two distinct types: social stigma is characterized by prejudicial attitudes and discriminating behaviour directed towards individuals with mental health problems as a result of the psychiatric label they have been given. In contrast, perceived stigma or self-stigma is the internalizing by the mental health sufferer of their perceptions of discrimination (Link, Cullen, Struening & Shrout, 1989), and perceived stigma can significantly affect feelings of shame and lead to poorer treatment outcomes (Perlick, Rosenheck, Clarkin, Sirey et al., 2001).

I was impressed by the Doctor not minding being interrupted while talking. I was soon to learn that this was the norm. I was quiet horrified to hear what some of these women went through before coming to the clinic. It was nothing short of verbal hostility. It was hard to imagine how they managed to cope with this abuse as long as they did.

Is it so difficult to understand that depression is an illness? Arrange for someone to order you to sober up once you have drunk down the contents of a bottle of brandy. Now that you are totally drunk, obey the order, "sober up now" can you do it, of course not, it's impossible. Well, that is how it is when a person is suffering depression. You cannot just snap out of it; just like you can't sober up now.

I suffer with depression, and while I was going to the gym for those three years, I hardly had any depressed days. I've learned a few pointers to get rid of depression: get out of the house, go walking, join a hiking club. If you are strapped for cash, get a few friends together or go by yourself, walk your neighbourhood. I greet the people I meet whilst walking my neighbourhood.

If you live near a wooded area which has a stream running through it; foot-cut your own trail. Get involved with you church youth or older group but keep your mind busy. But most of all join a Bible Study Group that has a strong prayer support group. Physical, mental and Spiritual health is a sure three way winner to combat depression. No, it may not go away, but by the Grace of God you will have victory over it more often, eventually you will develop a pattern which will help you to avoid it.

As for the stigma of depression, that some uninformed person has put on you; that too will pass, and you will feel a lot better. Remember, give thanks to God each day, He will give you victory, and the days you don't have victory, give thanks for that day. Let God know that you are thankful that He has reminded you that it was by His Grace that you had all the other days free of depression. As the depression lessons, so will you care less about the stigma and any side remarks you may hear about yourself.

We have an enemy that wants us to discredit our Heavenly Father. Those days we fall into depression are not from our Father, it is the enemy attacking us. Satan wants us to fail at being well again, but Our Heavenly Father lifts us up by His strength and our faith in Him, to be victorious over our depression.

Sadly I listened and watched as some of the women broke down and wept in our sessions with the different therapists. We are born cute cuddly babes, so where did we turn into these heartless trolls. Not only was it the women there that suffered humiliation, there were men as well. My personal experience is that the ones tormenting them were themselves weak but had not the courage to face it as these men and women had.

Listening but not yet ready to participate in the discussions, for I still had my own demons to deal with; and they had nothing to do with Lance's death. These were from another time, one could say another life. For I had grown away from that life I was raised up in and left it behind, so I thought. This Doctor was a man amongst men, he calmed the women and men and lifted their spirits before letting us break for tea, and a well-deserved cup, I might add.

My room was on the other side of the building. Having washed my face in cold water hoping to ease my throbbing head, naturally it did not help, it dawned on me that I had a headache powder in my suitcase somewhere...found it. Tea, a few biscuits and a sneaked powder, ten minutes later I felt fine, my head was much better.

On my way back to my room I passed the youth, I smiled at them and in a tone just loud enough for them to hear I said "Hi you bandits".

They had to laugh, oh boy just my luck, a very stern voice from behind me. "Mister Hillier, you know all too well that there is to be no communication between your group and the youth."

That voice had to belong to a very serious sergeant major type of matron half way to becoming a general; I turned around, there in the passage stood a lovely young Physiotherapist, my jaw dropped. No it's not possible that that lovely lady...nooo...no, she had such a sweet voice, I have heard her speaking, no, whoever yelled at me was long gone, they had to be, surly they had to be.

I collected my note book and headed back to the classroom, that is what I now called it, but just before I went around the corner down to the classroom, I checked to see that it was clear of the youth as well of the sergeant-major.

Turning the corner, one of the nurses came up behind me "Mister Hillier, I hope we aren't going to have any problems from you." I was floored, how did that little incident get around that fast I pondered? I would have to watch myself.

Being the first to arrive, I took my place in the back row again and waited. They arrived in one mass and the class was full, then the physiotherapist entered the room, singled me out with a quick death glance but said nothing, which would have been easy for her, I was the only one sporting a grey chinstrap beard.

She turned to the white board and wrote the words 'Boundaries in Relationships' on it. A little confused I tried to make sense of it, and then I twigged, I actually lived my life this way. Certain people in my life I kept at a distance, others I allowed them to get closer to me. As she spoke, a visualized a target with all its rings and the bulls eye in the middle, the bulls eye being me. Each ring going out from me had a group of people in it.

The ring immediately outside of me was for my wife. The first and second ring for my children and the rest were for other family members and friends as I felt I could trust them, and here the operative word is trust. One can have a best friend, but they have to earn ones trust.

I heard a young lady once say "She is my best friend because she is kind, caring, hates gossiping and loves sport and animals, but I can't trust her with a secret because she just blurts it out to everyone."

Then within that circle you find someone you can trust though they are not your best friend but close enough to be one. It all sound rather higgledy-piggledy, but that is how she does it, anyway, getting back to the matter at hand. A boundary is that space that is yours alone, the bulls' eye, the place where you feel safe and secure, where no one else but you alone reside.

In a healthy relationship no one is in control of the other person, both have a respect for each other and an understanding of the other's needs. They give each other time and space as needed, and look out for small ways to create happiness for the other person.

It often happens that when a relationship starts that boundaries are not set. This usually ends up in an unhappy situation where the stronger partner starts to try and dominate the relationship and the weaker retaliates. This pecking order soon leads to violence followed by words of humiliation. Many children learn insulting behaviour from parents or siblings, and see that aggression is the way to get what you want. Unfortunately some of the children in the family are quick to learn that the maddest dog gets the bone.

Boundaries are essential when a partner tries to invade one's space with intent to control physically or emotionally. At best, these invasions are done by bullying, manipulation or any other means possible, this is known as boundary transgression. Consider a mother who constantly wants affection from her married son regardless of the harm she is causing him to do to her grandchildren. Should he not set boundaries for her, he could cause emotional damage to his children that will come back to haunt him later in life. In other cases, we find that the weaker parent who submits to this invasion bares resentment and anger and in very few cases, even leads to the assault of the invading party and inevitably destroying the entire family.

You should never have to feel unsafe in a relationship. A good relationship is where both parties give each other the assurance that they are both emotionally and physically safe with them in that relationship. Trust is the key word here, trust in God, trust in each other, trust in oneself. Once these have been tested and proved successful, once each person is sure of the others love, then I would say ask for her hand. Never blame your partner for a mistake, look at the problem and direct the blame at the situation, not at the person.

My wife decided to cook rice shortly after we got married, she burnt it. Assessing the problem, it was concluded that if I had not disturbed her in the kitchen drawing her attention to my romantic desires, she would have noticed the water level dropping in the pot instead of fighting me off. Burnt rice never tasted so good.

To this day we do not blame each other for anything that goes wrong in the house, regardless of human error or not. Being married for more than forty years now, our boundaries are one, so much so that I'm too scared to think. We far too often have the same thoughts. I put it down to us reading the Bible and praying together every day for the same things and for our children.   It was this attitude that helped us help each other through the dark times, and be of strength for our children.

There was a short break before the next class. I snuck down to the lounge for a banana and then back to class. Most of the patients had stayed in their seats; I left my book on my chair. The therapist came in and stood before us, she had the daunting task of helping us deal with loss. I knew how I wanted to deal with my loss but I had to keep my promise to my son, my head began to hurt even more so now than it did five minutes ago. There is no formula for dealing with the loss of a loved one; we are all created with a different chip in us, that is we all have different ways of expressing our sorrow. On a larger platform we could be put into groups, but in a small room it posed an even greater challenge for our speaker. All-in-all said and done, she did well at covering the topic by making it interesting, being mindful too that there were patients from different religious backgrounds before her.

Being a Christian and having suffered loss on several occasions, friends, sisters, brother, parents and now a son, I know to whom to go. There are so many people in society who when faced with a loss feel lost. To them it is an end, there is no hope of ever seeing that person again, but that is not so. The Bible gives us Christians the truth of what is really to happen at the end of the world, it is so plain and clear.

I mentioned that I grew away from my past life, well, in that life I touched on card reading, Ouija board and séances, they are not the demons I was still to face. When doing these satanic things, we, yes I did them in a group with other people, we communicated with loved ones. Being young and very naïve, I believed in what I was doing. As I grew older and discovered the Bible, that all changed for me. I began to study the Holy Word for myself. At first it was no easy task, as time went by I found like-minded friends and we studied together.

Back in the day we did not have computers, the main source was the library and religious books that belonged to the old folks, I consumed these. I learnt that the best studies were the ones with the most Bible references. Then one day a group of men came to the church I had just joined, in their arsenal were two boxes, each box had twenty Bible Studies for the layman, I bought both. It is from these that I have chosen to share two studies, with texts that made me realise what I had got into as a young lad, my eyes were opened.

We all feel that emptiness when we lose a child, wife, husband, brother or sister and want to know if they suffered of not. There is nothing with such a request, after all we are human. The bottom line is they are laid to rest and no longer feel any pain. To dwell on such things and beat ourselves with that stick of self-concern over them is not what God intended for us. How many of us know what God has left for us in the Bible regarding those we have loved and lost? Not many at all. You may want to get your Bible to follow from here on.

Chapter 10

The following texts are also taken from the Old King James Bible as it is, to my mind, the most accurate translation of all the Bibles. As we go through these texts, it is my prayer that what I have thus far written, makes sense to you regarding the careful upbringing of our children in a loving Christian home.

Romans 6:23 "For the wages of sin is death; but the gift of God is eternal life through Jesus Christ our Lord."

Raising our children to know right from wrong, they must first know the founder of the Law – Jesus.

Genesis 3:4 "And the serpent said unto the woman, ye shall not surely die."

Here we find the first lie in the Bible directed to humanity, and it is Satan uttering it. This lie has been carried through the centuries and finally brought to us in the form of Spiritualism. Today we can find it in every town and city and in churches. My question is, why is it so rampant amongst the heathen tribes of Africa if it so 'religious'. Dead means dead.

Ezekiel 18:20 "The soul that sins, it shall die. The son shall not bear the iniquity of the father: neither shall the father bear the iniquity of son: the righteousness of the righteous shall be upon him, and the wickedness of the wicked shall be upon him."

We each carry our own cross and are held accountable for our own actions. We will still see this verse played out in Revelation when we cover the resurrections.

Genesis 2:7 "And the LORD God formed man of the dust of the ground, and breathed into his nostrils the breath of life; and man became a living soul."

This is a very interesting verse. Notice the last two words, living soul. If that dust, which became a living soul from God's breath, is not a seperate entity when it dies, how then can it go to Heaven when one dies? Why is it in a casket, would we not see it ascend heavenwards? The idea of going to heaven when we die is not true. We go to our graves and the breath goes back to God, there we stay until we hear the sound of the trumpet. In order to be risen up from the grave and then ascend to Heaven, we have to be immortal, so when does that take place if my body 'soul' is in the ground?

1 Corinthians 15:51-55 "Behold, I show you a mystery; we shall not all sleep, but we shall all be changed. In a moment, in the twinkling of an eye, at the last trump; for the trumpet shall sound, and the dead shall be

raised incorruptible, and we shall be changed. For this corruptible must put on incorruption, and this mortal must put on immortality. So when this corruptible shall have put on in- corruption, and this mortal shall have put on immortality, then shall be brought to pass the saying that is written, Death is swallowed up in victory. O death, where is thy sting? O grave, where is they victory? "

In the texts above we read of the sleep, being changed, being raised incorruptible and the last line, questioning the graves hold on the righteous after the resurrection. The big question is, how many resurrections are there going to be? This question we will look at a little later.

A Pharisee by the name of Nico-dē-mūs, a ruler of the Jews, who came to Jesus by night, admitted to Jesus that they knew He had to have come from God, because no man could do what He did without God being with Him John 3:1, 2 after some discussion, Jesus was asked by him how this was possible.

In verse 11-13 "Jesus answers him. Verily, verily, I say unto thee, We speak that we do know, and testify that we have seen; and ye receive not our witness. If I have told you earthly things, and ye believe not, how shall ye believe of heavenly things? And no man hath ascended up to heaven, but he that came down from heaven, even the Son of man which is in heaven."

Again I ask the question, how is it possible for our loved ones to be in Heaven?

If you recall how man was formed from the earth in Genesis, then God breathed into his nostrils the breath of life. Well in the book of Ecclesiastes we find out just what happens at the passing away.

Ecclesiastes 12:7 "Then shall the dust return to the earth as it was; and the spirit (or breath in Hebrew "Ruach) shall return unto God who gave it."

So how much do our dearly departed beloved ones know about us, are they here with us?

Ecclesiastes 9:5, 6 "For the living know they shall die; but the dead know not anything, neither have they anymore a reward; for the memory of them is forgotten. (After the earth has been made anew, God in his infinite mercy will remove the memory from the saved of the ones lost.) Also their love, and their hatred, and their envy, is now perished; neither have they anymore a portion forever in anything that is done under the sun."

They can no longer love, hate feel envy or have any part of life. As the text says, they know nothing. The soul has returned to dust and the spirit back to God.

To put it more plainly let us turn to the psalmist and see what David and Job also have to say on this matter.

Psalm 146:4 "His breath goes forth, he returned to his earth; in that day his thoughts perish."

Job 14:21 "His sons come to honour, and he knows it not; and they are brought low, but he perceives it not of them."

Believe it or not, but there are people who will argue that this is not true, that they have seen their loved ones and spoken to them, well, I do not dispute what they saw, but it was not their loved ones. This I will also cover from the Bible, and as shocked as I was then, maybe you will be too. The Bible holds only The Truth.

We have read of death and sleep and explained that death means dead and sleep mean to rest, but let us find out what kind of rest 'sleep' is referred to in the context of death. Jesus tells his disciples that Lazarus is sleeping.

John 11:14 "These things said he: and after that he said unto them, Our friend Lazarus sleeps; but I go, that I may awake him out of his sleep. Then said his disciples, Lord, if he sleep, he shall do well. How be it Jesus spoke of his death: but they thought he had spoken of rest in sleep. Then said Jesus unto them plainly, Lazarus is dead."

So, sleep also means dead, but in the broader frame of things, it fits in perfectly. We go to our graves to await the Lords coming and as mentioned in 1 Corinthians 15:51-55 we are changed, but the whole event does not end there, what about the second resurrection? But let us not get ahead of ourselves.

Why, why did I put this in my book? Because it gave us closure and the assurance that we would see our son again one day, it is not all over, kaput, finito, we raised him as a Christian. We know from people who saw him on that sad morning, that he looked peaceful, he was talking while sitting on a wall. We know to whom he was talking. We speak to Him every morning just as Lance did that morning, His name is Jesus... Jesus Christ... Our Saviour.

Don't give up; you do not know what went through your loved ones mind before they departed. Can you say for sure that your loved one never thought of Christ, never sat quietly contemplating going to church, said prayers, never had discussions of a religious nature with a friend or colleague, are you that sure?

Where did all this trouble start, why the deception? It's not all that difficult to see if we just take note of what is happening around us. Do I believe in predestination? Yes I do. Jesus Christ has predestined us for eternal life and Satan has predestined us for eternal death, but God does not force us, the choice is ours. I choose Jesus Christ's way. So where did it start, this terrible war for the lives of mankind.

Revelation 12:7-9 "And there was war in heaven: Michael and his angels fought against the dragon; and the dragon fought against his angels, and prevailed not; neither was there place found anymore in heaven. And the great dragon was cast out, that old serpent, called the Devil, and Satan, which deceives the whole world; he was cast out into the earth, and his angels were cast out with him."

There you have it, the devil decided to take revenge on God, deceive His creation, deceive them and drag them down with himself. Deceive them in any way possible; just get them to turn away from God, use any method to do so. The more of us they take away from God the greater the heartache they cause Him.

The devil is not a fool, he knows our weaknesses and zeros in on them, be it money, the want of power, to work deceptions, seeing our deceased loved ones, whatever it may be, he will give it to us, just to keep us away from serving Christ. But what is it worth? On a tomb stone are two dates, the date of birth and the date of departure with a dash between and it is that dash which represents the length of time we spent on earth. How we spend it is up to us, how we are judged is up to our Saviour Jesus Christ. That short dash of life will determine Heaven or Hell for us, we make that choice.

Let us at least help our children to make the right choices in life by our standards. That is by our Christian choices. On the day of the first resurrection we can have eternal life with Jesus. That to me is worth more than all the power, gold, popularity or anything else the devil can offer me. Life eternal for a dash.

As promised; let us look at what takes place at the second resurrection. A thousand years have gone by and the graves of the lost are opened by Jesus. The only explanation that I can give about the state of the dead is best left to the author of life, Jesus Christ.

Revelation 14:6-14 New King James Version (NKJV)

6 "Then I saw another angel flying in the midst of heaven, having the everlasting gospel to preach to those who dwell on the earth—to every nation, tribe, tongue, and people—"

7 saying with a loud voice, "Fear God and give glory to Him, for the hour of His judgment has come; and worship Him who made heaven and earth, the sea and springs of water."

8 "And another angel followed, saying, "Babylon[a] is fallen, is fallen, that great city, because she has made all nations drink of the wine of the wrath of her fornication."

9 "Then a third angel followed them, saying with a loud voice, "If anyone worships the beast and his image, and receives his mark on his forehead or on his hand,"

10 "he himself shall also drink of the wine of the wrath of God, which is poured out full strength into the cup of His indignation. He shall be tormented with fire and brimstone in the presence of the holy angels and in the presence of the Lamb."

11 "And the smoke of their torment ascends forever and ever; and they have no rest day or night, who worship the beast and his

image, and whoever receives the mark of his name."

12 "Here is the [b]patience of the saints; here[c] are those who keep the commandments of God and the faith of Jesus."

13 "Then I heard a voice from heaven saying [d]to me, "Write: 'Blessed are the dead who die in the Lord from now on."

14 "Yes," says the Spirit, "that they may rest from their labours, and their works follow them."

Revelation 20 New King James Version (NKJV)

Satan Bound 1,000 Years

20 "Then I saw an angel coming down from heaven, having the key to the bottomless pit and a great chain in his hand."

2 "He laid hold of the dragon, that serpent of old, who is the Devil and Satan, and bound him for a thousand years;"

3 "and he cast him into the bottomless pit, and shut him up, and set a seal on him, so that he should deceive the nations no more till the thousand years were finished. But after these things he must be released for a little while."

The Saints Reign with Christ 1,000 Years

4 "And I saw thrones, and they sat on them, and judgment was committed to them. Then I saw the souls of those who had been beheaded for their witness to Jesus and for the word of God, who had not worshiped the beast or his image, and had not received his mark on their foreheads or on their hands. And they lived and reigned with Christ for a thousand years."

5 "But the rest of the dead did not live again until the thousand years were finished. This is the first resurrection."

6 "Blessed and holy is he who has part in the first resurrection. Over such the second death has no power, but they shall be priests of God and of Christ, and shall reign with Him a thousand years."

Satanic Rebellion Crushed

7 "Now when the thousand years have expired, Satan will be released from his prison."

8 "and will go out to deceive the nations which are in the four corners of the earth, Gog and Magog, to gather them together to battle, whose number is as the sand of the sea."

9 "They went up on the breadth of the earth and surrounded the camp of the saints

and the beloved city. And fire came down from God out of heaven and devoured them."

10 "The devil, who deceived them, was cast into the lake of fire and brimstone where the beast and the false prophet are. And they will be tormented day and night forever and ever."

The Great White Throne Judgment

11 "Then I saw a great white throne and Him who sat on it, from whose face the earth and the heaven fled away. And there was found no place for them."

2 "And I saw the dead, small and great, standing before God, and books were opened. And another book was opened, which is the Book of Life. And the dead were judged according to their works, by the things which were written in the books."

13 "The sea gave up the dead who were in it, and Death and Hades delivered up the dead who were in them. And they were judged, each one according to his works."

14 "Then Death and Hades were cast into the lake of fire. This is the second death."

15 "And anyone not found written in the Book of Life was cast into the lake of fire."

Two resurrections; the first for those who lived a God fearing loving life to be raised up first to meet Jesus in the clouds where they will be escorted by Him and the angels to Heaven. There they will go through the books of life which will explain why there are lost souls still in their graves.

The second resurrection is for the lost souls who preferred not to heed God's warning via the Bible. They chose to be disobedient, they chose not to hear the voice of the Holy Spirit when He tried to turn them back onto the path of righteousness. They chose the way of the world and there for must suffer the consequences; to be burned up in the lake of fire and be no more.

Revelation 21:4, KJV "And God shall wipe away all tears from their eyes; and there shall be no more death, neither sorrow, nor crying, neither shall there be any more pain: for the former things are passed away."

Isaiah 25:8, KJV "He will swallow up death in victory; and the Lord GOD will wipe away tears from off all faces; and the rebuke of his people shall he take away from off all the earth: for the LORD hath spoken it."

Matthew 25:21, KJV "His lord said unto him, well done, thou good and faithful servant: thou hast been faithful over a few things, I will make thee ruler over many things: enter thou INTO THE JOY of thy lord."

Heaven can only permit those who have served God and the reason is:

1Cor.6 "Know ye not that the unrighteous shall not inherit the kingdom of God? Be not deceived: neither fornicators, nor idolaters, nor adulterers, nor effeminate, nor abusers of themselves with mankind,"

1 Corinthians 6:10

[10] "Nor thieves, nor covetous, nor drunkards, nor revellers, nor extortioners, shall inherit the kingdom of God."

In simple terms, sin will never enter into heaven again. Satan will have been destroyed, his angels and followers with him.

Personality and character are not taught, they are learned by observation our children watch us. As Jesus lived his life, live yours. "One sinner can destroy much good." Ecclesiastes 9:18.

Chapter 11

The rest of the afternoon passed without any incident at the clinic. I took a slow walk around the grounds and stopped off under tree just to listen to a bird calling to its mate. I was missing my family and could not wait for the weekend to see them. The loneliness was getting to me and before I knew it depression had set in. like a thief in the night, it snuck up on me, it hit me hard.

I went back to my room and had a good old fashioned cry, yeah I know, men don't cry, so what, I cry and I still do, Guess what? I'm in good company, John 11:35 Jesus wept, he wept because his heart went out to Mary and those who wept for the death of Lazarus. Jesus' groaned in the spirit and was troubled (John 11:33) freely showing his feelings to those who had lost a loved one. He felt no shame in openly expressing his emotions before Mary and the Jews who came with her.

I miss my son' maybe in time I will be able to think of him without the tears, but for now they are part of my healing process. I can speak freely to Morgan about him and he to me. We sometimes exchange a story or two but we are both at ease with the situation. Morgan knows that he will see his brother again, because he is living the life that Jesus has set out for us in His

Holy Word, plus he is keeping to His Ten Commandments.

Not so long ago my brother lost his son and I went to the funeral. It was so strange; because it was just over a year that I was at his wife's funeral, Wendy. Nathan was very close to his mom, he missed her very much after she died. He took to drinking to ease the pain of loss. When it came time to stop, he found it difficult to resist the temptation. We all know the old story, while you pay, you have pals, they were undeniably not out to help him stop drinking. Nathan was maybe too friendly and kind to his friends, but were they to him, who knows.

Looking back I can see Gods hand in it all. Me as a child, I heard my mother often pray for her children when she thought nobody was around. She would pray for all her children and grandchildren by name, I can quiet positively say that she did this from the time of her first born. We are a family who turn to God in times either good or bad. But speaking of my brother and myself, we both married women of prayer.

Wendy's eldest son, Patrick was in a financial bind one day, he came to his mother with his problem, as we all do. Her immediate response was did you pray about it? He had not, so off he went, whether he did or not I am not sure but I do know she did, she told me. The night before the amount was due, his wife held a show at their home. She sold garments directly to boutiques. They sold the exact amount that was due the next day. Patrick was over the moon, he could not wait to tell his mother. Here again I know that Wendy gave thanks on behalf of her son.

It all started with ouma's prayers for her children and grandchildren all those years before, then a mother's prayer for her children. I don't think Patrick has forgotten that experience. As for all my beautiful nieces, I hope they are praying for their children and grandchildren.

My brother, Walter, and I share the same grief. He being much older than me and surrounded by his daughter and family, might be the only thing that is keeping him together. I know too that this experience has made him see life in a different way and brought him closer to our Father in Heaven. It is said that the pen is mightier than the sword. Prayer is mightier than the pen, as the pen is mightier than the sword.

I'm not sure how I felt the next morning. I tried to get my head around what was presented in class about dealing with loss challenging my idea of coping with loss. I wrestled the night before to accept the general idea but it would not take. At breakfast I listened to some of the conversations around me, I was fortunate enough to catch the tail end of one discussion. The gentleman was saying that he felt a lot better after yesterday lesson on dealing with loss; that helped me to shelve the debate that was going on in my head.

Note book in hand, off I went to class for my new lesson. I was determined to attend as many lessons as possible to help me understand my problem and any other problems in the group. My idea was to listen in order to learn and understand, not to listen to question. Today's lesson was an important one for me; it was a mile stone on my way to recovery; linking Mental Health and Physical Health.

It all came together for me, as I mentioned before, I spent three years in a gym building muscle therefore understood mind power in the positive sense. Forgive me for repeating myself here, Spiritual, physical and mental health are the key to a healthy life. I put a lot of emphasis on spiritual and mental exercise such as prayer, reading the Bible, praying for other people's needs. By praying for others, one tends to forget one's own problems for a while allowing time for healing. Why not enjoy a quiet time of meditation by focusing on scripture; or sitting in a secluded place, listening to a piece of religious music portraying Christ. I enjoy being in a garden reading my Bible. The best time for me is to be at the sea, listening to the waves and speaking to my Saviour.

After having checked the program after class, I decided to take a break until the afternoon. My head was still hurting quite a bit, so much so that I did not feel like being around people, my temper was scratchy and I was tired. I had been this way for a long time. My patience was growing thin with waiting to see my psychiatrist. I knew that a wrong word or some silly action from someone could set me off, so I put myself under room arrest until I had simmered down.

At last lunch time, with my rumbling tummy, my hurting head and irritability, I went to lunch and truly enjoyed it, the pudding as well. Refreshed after drinking two glasses of apple juice, I must admit my head felt a lot better and my mood had changed drastically. Off to class to hear a presentation by the therapist on 'how I interpret things'. This I had to hear. I'm just a man and when it comes to women I get it all wrong and befuddled. I think I can count the number of times I got it right on one hand with a finger or two to spare.

I don't remember the lesson all that clearly, but do have the gist of it. I recall a friend of mine from my school days being blasted by a girl he liked, I mean drooled over. A few weeks later there they were, hand in hand, my brain went all fuzzy and did summersaults. I knew that after that 'in-your-face' get lost loser, there was no way she would ever go out with him. What happened I asked them? She said that he could not just out with his 'I love you' emotions for her in front of her friend like that; it embarrassed her to no end. He should have realized that the time was not right and waited. He thought it was the best time because her friends were there to hear how he felt!

One morning I wanted to go fishing with a friend. My girlfriend had come around to visit me. I asked her if it was alright with her if I went fishing for a few hours, she said I could go. I went fishing for a few hours while she visited with my sister. When I returned home, boy did I get and ear full. But you said I could go. Now catch this line, you should have taken notice of the tone of my voice, I meant no. why not just say so. Man, that was the coldest most silent summer afternoon of my entire life; I was too scared to even breathe too loudly in her company should I arouse her attention that I was there and get a second round of hot air.

Interpreting situations and words, how are we supposed to do that when we do not expect anything to happen? On his last visit to us, Lance gave all the signs of saying goodbye and we did not pick them up. Because we do not expect the worst of our children, that is why. By the worst, I mean, doing themselves harm. We are members of The Companionate Friends (TCF) that is where we learnt of the tell-tail signs. If you are asking why did I not see the signs, it is because you, like us and most of the others did not expect the worst thing to happen to your child. It is not your fault. It would have happed even if you had seen the signs. I am not a psychiatrist. Having listened to the learned in this field, I know enough to know that once they reach that point of no-return, we can no longer help them. Help them spiritually, that we can do. We did not cover this in the class, this I learnt at my TCF group meeting.

I still had some time before seeing my psychiatrist, the thought of a nice cup of tea and a biscuit sounded just peachy, after which I went for a slow walk amongst the trees. I listened to the birds calling to each other. Is it not wonderful, birds tell their story in song; they share it with all who take the time to stop and listen to them.

Contemplate this saga, politicians sit around a table to discuss peace, this one wants more land, that one wants more gold, the other more power and so on. Birds on the other hand own the heavens, trees, land and rivers. Like us, there are a variety of them, they share the earth with each other and never go to war, with the exception of the birds of prey. Every morning they greet the new day in song and close the day with excited chatter. I'm sure they are all trying to tell each other of their day's events, and the mother bird telling the chicks it is time to sleep.

Ever heard of a bird dropping a bomb on its neighbours nest? Every day I hear Politian's talking of a brighter future; I am living in my future and it is not bright. The bird's life has never changed, that is why they can sing their story to their friends.

When Jesus comes, it will all change, only then will my family and I have a brighter future with those of you who cling to Jesus Christ and His Word. Where peace will reign forever, where sickness will never be known, where death will have been conquered and life will be eternal under the government of the Father, Son and Holy Spirit. Believe me when I tell you this, there will be many surprises waiting for us, members of families who departed by their own hand will be there all because they knew Jesus and their families never knew about their relationship with Him. Would it not be wonderful to find a family member tap you on the shoulder and say, "Glad you could make it." The flip side is a sad side. The family member, who took their own life makes it, but you refused to take hold of Jesus' hand.

In the book of Revelation, John is in vision.

Revelation 21:3-4.

"And I heard a great voice out of heaven saying, Behold, the Tabernacle of God is with men, and he will dwell with them, and they shall be his people, and God himself shall be with them, and be their God.

And God shall wipe away all tears from their eyes: and there shall be no more death, neither sorrow, nor crying, neither shall there be any more pain: for the former things are passed away."

In order to understand the sincerity of what Christ is saying, read Revelation chapters 18 – 22.

Chapter 12

What I have written here is from a church bulletin. It was written by Ron Hutchcraft, I am not sure when but it sums up chapters 18 to 22, of Revelation, beautifully. Ron has his own ministries and can be found on Google.

"Winning the animal battle with the animal inside"

"Several years ago on an Indian reservation, a friend there told us about an elderly neighbour of hers who had taken an unusual pet into her home - It was half wolf, half dog. Half wild, half domestic, dig trouble.

One morning that wolf-dog picked up the lady's granddaughter and began to carry it away. The grandmother saw it, she screamed at the top of her lungs. The animal stopped and froze in this moment of evident struggle between his wild and tame side.

The wolf-dog looked straight at the screaming lady, totally unafraid; his wild side wasn't scared at all. His wild side wanted that child for food. Suddenly in one dramatic moment the animal dropped the child, the domestic side of the animal won over."

As humans, we are all too familiar to this pattern, we know just how strong they both are within us. Romans 7:15 Paul the Apostle says, "what I want to do I do not do, but what I hate I do."

Galatians 5:16 -17. "This I say then, Walk in the Spirit, and ye shall not fulfil the lust of the flesh.

For the flesh lusts against the spirit, and the Spirit against the flesh: and these are contrary one to the other: so that ye cannot do the things he would."

Whichever way you choose will be the deciding factor of your final fate. Revelation 21:7 "He that overcomes shall inherit all things; and I will be his God, and he shall be my son."

Revelation 21:8 "But the fearful, and unbelieving, and the abominable, and murderers, and whoremongers, sorcerers, and idolaters, and the liars, shall have their part in the lake which burns with fire and brimstone; which is the second death."

'But the fruits of the Spirit are love, joy, peace, long suffering, patience, kindness, goodness, faithfulness, gentleness and self-control.' Those who belong to Jesus Christ have surrendered their carnal nature to Him. We have no power over our animal nature, therefor without Christ's help we become like animals in our behaviour.

Daniel was a captive in Babylon, yet three times a day he prayed to God for strength Daniel 6:10. It is only by His power that we are saved, reach out and take His hand, by taking His hand you can lead your family as you follow Jesus. Who wants to behave like an animal when there is so little time left to enjoy.

If you had two dogs, one black, one white and you set them against each other, who would win the fight? There is a story that Billy Graham told of a fisherman. Every weekend he would bring his dogs to town and take bets as to who would win, the fisherman made a lot of money. One day he was asked by a friend how he knew which dog would win. His answer was simple, I feed one more than the other for that week, the stronger one wins. So it is with our nature, feed one and the other loses. As I mentioned earlier, children learn from watching their parents, know your choice.

Chapter 13

My time with my psychiatrist was emotional for me. We dealt with my depression and headaches. It concerned him that I had so many headaches and booked me for a scan. I left his office with a script in hand to be handed in at the medical post, which I did. That night at dinner I saw my fate sitting at the table for the addicts. She had a white cap on her head and a multitude of wires tied together leading off her head down to a small black box at her side. She looked like an escaped alien from the planet coo-coo; I was to be the next escapee, there were to be many more during my stay there. This we wore for twenty four hours to record our brain activity. This is where they discovered I had epileptic brain seizures.

Blood pressure and temperature please, Mister Hillier, became an evening ritual. I was still keeping to myself, rude maybe, but then I was the one with a problem. What I did notice, all the new comers were doing the same thing, casing out the joint and the inmates; listening to what they spoke about, were they gossiping, trying to help or just friendly. While there I never heard of one bad encounter, amazing seeing that we were all emotionally unbalanced, until our medication started to take effect that is. People came and went every day, every day we saw new faces be it one or be it three.

I was off to class when I heard my name being called to report to the medical station, my meds had arrived, my first dose was waiting for me. I am as straight as a die, but I almost kissed the chap when I saw my pills, I was on track to recovery, really on track now. I noticed a slight spring in my depressed slow sluggish steps, my heart felt somewhat uplifted. I turned around and went back to my room, I was crying from joy. A while later, recomposed, I went down to class. The subject: Emotional Balance and Relationship.

It is not always easy to understand or appreciate the emotional needs of another person. It's as difficult as trying to find your lost car keys in a dark room. There is also the ability to let go, by this I mean giving that individual room, trusting in that person. We need to accept the other person's mistakes, be able to forgive and be big enough to ask for forgiveness in a relationship, this I believe to be a major part of emotional balance.

Becoming frustrated or angry while our partner remains calm does not help our balance of emotions within our relationships. Noting the calm response of one's partner and falling in line with it is the best solution of having a balanced emotional relationship. On the other hand, should one lose control of one's emotions in a balanced relationship, the partner should overlook the incident as an emotional outburst or deviation and move forward without holding any antipathies.

Emotional balance in relationships is not only the capability to control your own emotions and voice them appropriately, but it also means being able to understand the emotions of the other and acting accordingly.

What most people do not know, and what we are not taught in schools is that emotional balance is at the heart of every good healthy relationship. We need to be emotionally involved with each other, without it there is no bonding. To get that balance right is not easy.

The secret is to listen intensively to each other and pray together. It is while we listen to our partners prayers that we hear what it is that they want God to help us with, so listen, listen and ask God to change you. Ask him to help you boost that relationship into a Healthy Godly Relationship. Pray with your children in a family circle and do not feel uncomfortable if your partner asks God to help you in a certain area. Children need to hear that mom and dad need God's help in their lives, they will learn to ask God for help from you. This way you will have more emotional achievement and less emotional detachment. A happy wife or husband, a happy life.

Please bear in mind, all that is being mentioned in this book is to help you cope with loss, help those who feel lost and to try to prevent those who are contemplating suicide from committing the act.

You may say "what about me, I lost my loved one in an accident and now I am all alone in the world?" Truly, you are not all alone. You may be an only child and the last surviving member of your family. Think of the troops who came back from the Second World War. The British and Japanese soldiers who found their homes bombed and their families all gone. Try putting yourself in their shoes, the emotional distress of the war and then returning home to no emotional support at all: yet they survived, met someone, got married, had children, had grandchildren and lived a full life. How did they manage to overcome it all.

You have the chance to turn to Jesus. He suffered all the anguishes of being alone in the Garden of Gethsemane when his disciples failed to support him. Call on him for support and if you have not yet met him, read the books of Matthew, Mark, Luke and John. After that go through the Book of Psalms, and see how David relates his relationship with Jesus to us.

Let us take a step closer to home. The children's home for orphans. How many orphans do you know today as grown adults with children and grandchildren? I'm sure you do not know many if not none at all; that is because they don't live in the past. Getting up is the toughest part of it all, but getting up is where we start a new life. Starting a new life means meeting new people, not the kind that helped us get to where we were, but the type that will lift us up to a higher level.

How do I make that happen when I am so down and out? By using music to help me get into a positive frame of mind, a positive mind will help me project a positive aura that will draw positive people and not dropouts that do not want to be lifted up. Should you attract a down and out person who wants to be positive, help them to become positive, pass it on. The reason you attracted them is because they too want to be out of that rut. Pay it forward.

How do I become positive to attract positive people and not go back to where I was? Music, music is the key that is going to be part of your therapy to help you. It will help you project a positive image to attract positive people who will lift you up and not attract negative people who do not want to be lifted up. Be warned, you will be criticised by your old friends, ignore them. We are going to cover music therapy, read on.

We talk about healthy relations, we have mentioned prayer in a relationship, is there more to a healthy emotional relationships, yes there is;

The five languages of love.

1.   Words of Affirmation.

2.   Quality time.

3.   Receiving Gifts.

4.   Acts of Service.

5.   Physical Touch.

Let us start with words of affirmation, let's us ask Solomon what he has to say about the subject in (Proverbs 18:21) Death and life are in the power of the tongue: Both men and woman need to be appreciated and a man needs to let her know that by giving her compliments or showing his appreciation to her that he loves her and so women to men. A simple compliment, your hair looks great; thanks I needed that cup of tea. We need not go overboard. Wow you look great in that dress. I don't know how you do it, but you always know when I'm down and then you make me laugh and I feel better, thank for that. A sincere loving comment on how your spouse looks will keep them looking good for you.

Secondly spend quality time together. Pack a small picnic basket and go to the park together, leave the kids with grandma. Take her and the kids for an ice-cream and do window shopping together. Be the man, make tea and ask her to come and sit at the table alongside you, now ask her about her day and listen to her, be sure that the radio and telly are off. Converse with her during her telling you about her day, do it quietly, touch her hand every now and then. Every so often give her / him space to be alone. Time is a precious commodity, as I mentioned before, all it is, is a dash between to dates. Keep love alive.

All men and women love receiving gifts, it can be costly if you want it to be. A gift need not be extravagant, it can be less costly yet have a great deal of sentimental value. I bought my wife a Bible case, it was not that expensive and she bought me a cravat. You may be able to buy her a diamond ring and she may be able to buy you a car. The idea is that giving gifts is part of the big five; it shows the other person that you are thinking of them. When I go to the shop for my wife, I usually buy her a small chocolate, just to let her know I was thinking of her. Be mindful of your partner's needs. Keep love alive.

We also have acts of service, I mean doing things you know your spouse would like you to do. Consider actions such as cooking a meal, setting a table, emptying the dishwasher, vacuuming, changing the baby's diaper, picking up a prescription, keeping the car in operating condition; they are all acts of service. They require thought, planning, time, effort and energy. If done with a positive spirit, they are indeed expressions of love, "actions speak louder than words." When he is cutting the grass, serve him a cool-drink. Should he be doing maintenance on the car, make a few of his favourite sandwiches and a cup of tea. If she is having a quiet time alone, make her a cup of tea and take it to her, but do not speak, do not disturb her. Keep the love alive.

We have long known that physical touch is a way of communicating emotional love. Numerous research projects in the area of child development have made that conclusion: Babies who are held, stroked and kissed develop a healthier emotional life than those who are left for long periods of time without physical contact. Holding hands, kissing, embracing and sexual intercourse are all ways of communicating emotional love to one's spouse. Without it, they feel unloved. With it, their emotional tank is filled, and they feel secure in the love of their spouse. Divorce is not even in their minds but a long loving life together. Keep love alive.

Because my wife is some years older than me, I make a point of putting my arm around her waist or shoulder when in public. I hold her hand when walking in the mall. When we sit down to a meal in a restaurant, I hold her hand when saying grace silently or quietly. I make her feel special and I want the world to know she is special to me.

What of the man? He needs to know that his wife loves him even though she is older. Her friends will be older, she needs to make him not only feel; but let him know that he has a special place among them. Keep the love live.

As promised, what is music therapy and what is not? There are a many classes of music such as religious, classical, jazz, soul, bluegrass, rock, metallic, country and many others. We are only interested in those which the Music Therapy Association supports, because it is the only professional researched-based discipline that actively applies supportive science to the creative, emotional, and energizing experiences of music for health treatment and educational goals.

A music therapist is not someone off the street who thinks they can do the job, not at all. You have to spend many years studying and practising. Following case studies and analysing the results; one has be qualified in this field; people's emotions are at stake.

This question comes from the USA Medical Journal; quote Music therapists must have a bachelor's degree or higher in music therapy from one of AMTA's 72 approved colleges and universities, including 1200 hours of clinical training. Music therapists must hold the MT-BC credential, issued through the Certification Board for Music Therapists, which protects the public by ensuring competent practice and requiring continuing education. Some states also require licensure for board-certified music therapists. Music Therapy is an evidence-based health profession with a strong research foundation. Music Therapy degrees require knowledge in psychology, medicine, and music.

1. The following examples of therapeutic music are noteworthy, but are not clinical music therapy:

A person with Alzheimer's listening to an iPod with headphones of his/her favourite songs

Groups such as Bedside Musicians, Musicians on Call, Music Practitioners, Sound Healers, and Music Thanatologists

Celebrities performing at hospitals and/or schools

A piano player in the lobby of a hospital

Nurses playing background music for patients

Artists in residence

Arts educators

A high school student playing guitar in a nursing home

A choir singing on the paediatric floor of a hospital

2.	Finally, here are examples what credentialed Music Therapists do:

Have worked with a Congresswoman to regain her speech, after surviving a bullet wound to her brain.

Work with older adults to lessen the effects of dementia.

Work with children and adults to reduce asthma episodes.

Work with hospitalized patients to reduce pain.

Work with children who have autism to improve communication capabilities.

Work with premature infants to improve sleep patterns and increase weight gain.

Work with people who have Parkinson's disease to improve motor function.

In my case I listen to classical music to settle me down when my temper rises due to my headaches. It calms me then I am able to cope with people again. At best I do not like being around people, never have but for my family, as they understand me. When does my temper rise up other than because of my headaches? When I see children being ill-treated, when I see a women being badly treated or see it on the news. Our world is so full of mucho men that it makes me sick; in my book men are those who have an emotional balance with their wives, fiancé or girlfriend and sisters, that' a man. A real man only lifts his hand in front of his wife when she cannot reach an item above her and he steps in to help her.

I listen to music when I write; it helps keep my mind focused on the subject. Even when driving a car; I play music, religious, classical, Neil Diamond, that class of music. Has it helped my brain seizures, yes it has, I still get them, but the anger that accompanies it is not so fierce anymore. When I feel my mood wanting to change into a negative mood, I put on my head phones and listen to Vivaldi's Four

Seasons or any of the classic's; in no time at all my mood changes back to a pleasant one. There is a smile on my face, I feel light on my feet again and happy with the world. Music therapy plays a great part in my life and will continue to until the last hour of my life.

Music is a universal language, every person on earth can respond to it. A couple in love will want to hear love songs while a person who is studying will want to hear some light classical. One who is doing physical training will want to hear up-beat music to motivate them.

Music has it place in every part of our lives. Play Brahms Lullaby's to a baby to help the little one sleep. In a nutshell, music has an effect on our brains, it interacts with our emotional brain waves. That is why it is so important to be careful of what we choose to listen to. Music is a powerful tool in both right and wrong hands.

A study was done on a group of nursery school children. Music Therapists fitted speakers under the floor boards of the children's sleep room the day before. When it came time for the children to rest they played soothing music. All the music was instrumental; none of the music used had words to them. The children, after an active morning in the playground, quickly settled down.

The decibels were set low, the music played for a set time then changed drastically to an upbeat piece of music. With the change the children's mood began to change; they became rowdy, and picked on each other. Before it got out of hand, the music was switched back to the soothing classical piece again; the children settled down and were allowed to have their afternoon nap. During the entire time of this experiment, the teachers weren't present, but were watching from the next classroom via a monitor that had been set up to catch the outcome on film for the purpose of studying music therapy, they were astonished at the effect music has.

The power of music is ever reaching in all circumstances. Take the sinking of the Titanic, the musicians played 'Nearer my God to Thee' while all others scrambled to the life boats. When questioned about the sinking, the survivors, cold, traumatised and believing it all to be a bad dream, would start with "they played nearer my God to thee, they just stood there stood there." Godly music has a way of filling the heart with Godly strength as it did for King David when he faced off Goliath. David's heart was filled with Godly music and praise for our Father in Heaven. Make quiet Godly music a part of your home and fill your heart with it. Fill the hearts of your family and visitors with it. Ask Jesus to come and live in your home. He will send His Spirit, The Holy Spirit, to your home and Angels will accompany Him. While heavenly music is being played, love and peace will reign in your home.

Part 4

Chapter 14

Life after death.

My time at the clinic had come to an end. I had worked through my emotions and my medication had been arranged to help me cope with everyday life.

As I drove away from the clinic, I felt unsure of myself. I knew then that I had changed; I was no longer the same person I was a few months ago. Back then I was energetic and alive. Now I felt tired and as though half the life was sucked out of me. At the same time I knew I could not let this interfere with my family life, I still had children and a wife.

So many questions went through my mind. The only way I was to get real peace would be to find answers to these questions. That is when I started to find them.

I read Medical Journals; Doctors reports on behaviour but most of my answers came from the Bible. I was so amazed at how many answers I got to my questions; almost all of them I found the answers to in the Bible. Having done that, I decided to share my finding with parents who have lost a child.

Having God's peace is to have absolute peace. His word is truth and we have all the truth we need in His Word. He understands our emotions and feels our pain. When we go to Him, He is able to comfort us. Who comforted Our Heavenly Father when He saw His only begotten son dying on the cross? Who gave Him words of comfort? Who held His hand? Upon whose shoulder did He rest His head? No one, He stood alone. The awesome love that He has for us is that He will not let us, who believe in Him, face grief alone. His Spirit surrounds us (The Holy Spirit) and through Him we find piece.

Tragedies bring us closer to God, as do our fears. Once we have this peace, what do we do with it? We share it with those who have lost a loved one, be it a father, mother sister or brother. By sharing the peace of God we renew and strengthen the peace in us.

Read 1 Corinthians 13 every day to have a true experience of Our Fathers love.

John 14:27 "Peace I leave with you, my peace I give unto you: not as the world gives, give I to you. Let not your heart be troubled, neither let it be afraid."

You cannot find Jesus' peace in the world; He imparts that peace from His heart to yours.

Ephesians 1: 14 "He is our peace."

Those who love and obey Jesus have peace in their hearts.

Colossians 3:15 "And let the peace of God rule in your hearts..."

When calling on Jesus to live in our hearts He brings His peace and instils it in our hearts. James 3:18 "And the fruit of righteousness is sown in peace of them that make peace."

Many times in this book I refer to having impressions; these impressions come from my dear friend The Holy Spirit. He has helped me find the answers that troubled me and I know them to be true,

because they were revealed in the Scriptures of Jesus Christ. He also helped me write this book after much praying.

Obeying the Ten Commandments of God is the beginning of inner peace.

Chapter 15

Proverbs 20:7 "The just man walks in his integrity: his children are a blessing after him."

What a joy to have our sons and daughters follow after us in our integrity. This does not only apply to the men, the mothers have a great part in the upbringing of the children. One partner can destroy the other partner's integrity pulling the children down with them. That is why we covered emotional balance in a relationship first before child upbringing.

Proverbs 22:6 "Train up a child in the way he should go: and when he is old, he will not depart from it."

A house build with bricks is fairly strong, but one joined with mortar is very strong. We are the bricks of the house, Jesus is the mortar, he holds us all together as one. When a storm is seen on the horizon, we come together as a family; we kneel down and dad prays to our Saviour for protection. We hear dad asking Jesus to protect us children and mom; to keep us safe, then dad says to Jesus "Lord, please give me wisdom and courage to face the storm." There isn't a storm that can blow our house down, because my dad has Jesus on his side.

Psalms 34:7 "The angel of the Lord encamped about them that fear him, and delivered them."

One day when I'm all grown up and have my own family, I want to be like my dad. I want to be strong like him and not afraid to face any storm. For now, I'm watching how he does it so that I can do it just like him; and protect my family with Jesus's help.

Proverbs 20:11 "Even a child is known by his doings, whether his work be pure, and whether it be right."

What a joy to hear children speak these words of their parents in such a way. To know that there are children brought up in this manner sheds a ray of light across this dark world. Poverty, selfishness and greed for attention have robbed many children of love and happiness.

Many are taught that to get on in life they have to fight for everything. This advice leads to being unloved by those around them. If that does not work, steal, cheat or trample on heads, but get to the top; do whatever it takes but get there. What they are not told is that one day it all ends; pension day will come along and take away all the high status they thought would never end.

The 5th Commandment – Honour thy mother and father, is no longer being taught in the world today. A child can sue their parents. Have them arrested and who knows what else. Governments have lost sight of the big picture; Jesus is coming and how will we as leaders stand before him. So many don't even care what happens to our youth. I want you to know that a new government is going to rule this world. A government that has each one of us at their heart, the government of Jesus Christ, you have to be there, with your family, it is going to be heavenly peaceful.

Matthew 5:9 "Blessed are the peacemakers: for they shall be called the children of God."

To leave an everlasting mark on people's heart is for you to make that mark. It is made with kindness, caring, sacrifice and silent dedication to the wellbeing of others. You may think that nobody is watching, you think incorrectly dear friend. You have been noticed, it may be by a colleague in the office, factory or whatever work place you are in, but most of all; God has noticed your silent dedication to His praise.

Psalms 128:1 "Blessed is everyone that fears the Lord; that walks in his way."

Following Christ is not an easy task to take on but a highly rewarding one. The road to redemption is filled with problems. For those of you who have made the choice to follow Christ, Satan is not going to sit back and take your decision lying down, he is going to fight tooth and nail for your soul. He never wants to lose to his adversary Jesus Christ.

The truth is he has lost the war. He was cast out of Heaven and wants to keep you out as well.

Revelation 12:7-9 "And there was war in heaven: Michael and his angels fought against the dragon; and the dragon fought and his angels, 8 And prevailed not; neither was their place found any more in heaven. 9 And the great dragon was cast out, that old serpent, called the Devil, and Satan, which received the whole world: he was cast out into the earth, and his angels were cast out with him."

Press on; press on, on your knees praying for the Holy Spirit to enter into your life. The mightiest men and women, in the Bible, are to be found on their knees, so are the mightiest father's and mother's to be found there.

Psalms 12:3 "Thy wife shall be as a fruitful vine by the sides of your house: thy children like olive plants about thy table."

What a promise for a husband to hold onto when praying for his wife. How can one not want to follow our Lord Christ Jesus when there are so many promises in the Bible for us to claim as our own? Find them and teach them to the children. We do this in our home and in our church. Starting with the little ones builds character and faith in our Saviour Jesus. Whenever something good happens in their little lives, point to Jesus as the one who made it happen, build their faith in Him. It may happen that one day the burdens of life become too heavy for them to bear; they will remember their friend and turn to Him as did my son, as did Samson.

Psalms 128:6 "Yea, thou shall see thou children's children, and peace upon Israel."

Here is another of the many promises that we can hold fast too. Promises we can claim when that sweet hour of prayer comes around. Gathering our family together and reading stories of encouragement to them from the Bible. Another way to have family worship with small children is to find prayers in the Psalms, words of wisdom from Proverbs or the life of Christ in the four Gospels.

When that sweet hour of prayer comes around; it should be just that, a sweet hour of prayer. Keep the prayers short and to the point, children do not have a long attention time span, but for stories they do have, so use the time reading stories to them from the Bible. There is a set of Bible Stories available on the net 10 – 12 books. They will always remember the wonderful times, sitting around dad' or mom's feet listening to them reading stories to them.

Matthew 19:14 "...suffer little children and suffer them not, to come unto me, for such is the kingdom of heaven."

As tired as Jesus was, he would not turn children away. He always made time for them, an example to all working parents. We come home from work, tired and somewhat frustrated from a busy day at work. Think how Jesus felt day after day trying to teach his disciples humility and patience. At the end of the day the children delight in seeing their parents, make that time a joyful time for them, give them your time. You will have time later to sit back and relax, but now they want you, share their delight in whatever they show you that they did at school that day.

To give them of your time is to show them love, when you tell them that Jesus listens to them, they will believe you because of your example. Before leaving work for home, ask Jesus to help you be cheerful at work and when you get home, put on some soft Christian music in the car and get your mind in tune.

Matthew 11:28 "Come unto me, all ye that labour and are heavy laden, and I will give you rest."

Proverbs 16:32 "He that is slow to anger is better than the mighty; and he that rules his spirit than he that takes a city."

Ephesians 5:6 "Let no man deceive you with vain words: for because of these things cometh the wrath of God upon the children of disobedience."

The world has turned in on itself. There was once a time when men could be looked up to as upright gentlemen, but today they have become lovers of self. It is difficult to find a man true to himself. One who cannot be swayed by vain words. Liars, cheats are two cents a dozen, but an honest man is hard to find.

An honest man is one to look up to and be admired. Where such a man is found, families do just that, they look up to him. Proverbs 22:1 "A good man is rather to be chosen than great riches... "

Ephesians 5:7 "Be not ye therefore partakers with them."

Stepping to one side of the crowd is to be seen as different, separating one's self from the pack so to speak. Those who have chosen a life of sin will not want you around, you tend to show them up and that irritates them.

Proverbs 29:27 "an unjust man is an abomination to the just: and he that is upright is an abomination to the wicked." Your children will also notice the coldness from their friends, not being invited to parties, sleep overs and outing. Look at this as a golden opportunity to explain to them why it is so. Read to them the life of Noah, Abraham, Joseph, David, these were men on the outside.

There are many that put aside the social life and found true happiness.

Let your children know the truth that they are not welcome because they show up their friends sins. It is much better for us to have our own party or outing with like-minded friends who will be a blessing to us as we are to them.

Ephesians 5:8 "For ye were sometimes darkness, but now are ye light in the lord: walk as children of the light." Strengthening our children in Christ Jesus is an on-going task, one we may never let up on. Keep them in the light of the scriptures. Regardless of how old our children become.

Consider the prodigal son, Luke 15:11- 32, he left the presence of his father and went off into the world. Our children do the same thing today, so what's new. They want to experience the world, thinking they are strong enough to do so. Sadly, few ever return home, the world is too powerful for them and swallows them up. Our only hope is that the Biblical grounding we gave them will hold them together during the tough times. Those who return, they are here to stay.

For some it might be that for their children who do return, receive them with open arms and love them, no preaching, leave the past in the past. Give thanks to our Almighty Father for their return and for those of us who have lost a children, we give thanks for the time we had with them.

At The Companionate Friends meeting, we each lit a candle for a lost loved one, my wife and I lit one for Lance. We lit it in memory of him, not because we believe he is somewhere watching over us, no, because we want his memory to live on, as do the other member do for their loved ones. It is a lovely gesture and welcomed by all.

Try and think of heaven, no trains, aeroplanes, trucks, boats, mechanical noises, in fact no noises at all bar the sounds of heaven. Much singing from birds, people and all in tune: and all living in absolute peace and harmony. No debts to worry about at the months end, no illness, colds or flu or Politician's telling us lies. The only government will be the Father, Jesus and the Holy Spirit, and they have one mind.

I have family whom I want to see in heaven after the second resurrection, a baby sister that died at birth, a son, my parents, my in-laws and others. Come Lord Jesus come. When we follow Jesus Christ and labour for Him, we walk as children of light. Get the children to write out Bible texts and distribute them in mail boxes. Receiving Bible texts in a child's hand is always a pleasant surprise; you will be astonished how people will appreciate it. At the same time it teaches them that giving is so rewarding.

Many people think that when a person dies they go straight to heaven. Some believe in a place called Purgatory. Then there are those that believe they can contact the dead. As a child I heard many sermonettes besides an open grave on this subject to give the living peace of mind. But as I grew up and took an interest in the Bible, because of my mother, I found these words to be untrue.

In the past suicide was deemed a sin and the deceased were condemned to hell. Did the church know what went through the mind of that person just before following through. Today the Christian world has reversed its thinking and so has society, hence The Compassionate Friends, which is an organisation to be found almost all over the world to help grieving parents and siblings. They are there for any cause of death and a stronger support group you will not find anywhere else as they have suffered your loss and can relate to you.

It pains me to know that there are ministers who avoid the truth as it is written in the Holy Scriptures about the state of the dead. As i studied the scriptures i found many other areas where the truth has been overlooked.

Read your Bible, become familiar with its passages and promises and learn of my friend Jesus Christ.

I have shared my experience with you in faith that you may have blessed hope should you have to face such devastating new as we did; in the future. The only way to deal with it is through Jesus Christ and His Word. As you have read, I only used Bible texts to back my statements and that from the King James Version. Where I have shared the state of the dead with you is what the Bible, your Bible, teaches, not my ideas or what I think happens after death. May our Father in Heaven, our Saviour Jesus

Christ and The Holy Spirit be with you always as you make your decision to follow them and lead your children in their light for their salvation.

Chapter 16

The following texts are also taken from the Old King James Bible. As we go through these texts on the state of the dead, it is my prayer that what I have thus far written, makes sense to you regarding the careful upbringing of our children in a loving Christian home.

Romans 6:23 "For the wages of sin is death; but the gift of God is eternal life through Jesus Christ our Lord."

Geneses 3:4 "And the serpent said unto the woman, ye shall not surely die."

Here we have the first lie in the Bible committed by Satan himself, who from this point became the father of lies. This lie has been carried through the centuries and finally brought to us in the form of spiritualism. Today it is practiced n every city; and many churches. My question is, why is it so important amongst the heathen tribes of Africa and other parts of the world, if it is so religious. All said and done, dead means lifeless.

Ezekiel 18:20 "The soul that sins, it shall die. The son shall not bear the iniquity of the father; neither shall the father bear the iniquity of the son: the righteousness of the righteous shall be upon him, and the wickedness of the wicked shall be upon him."

We each carry our own cross and are responsible for our own actions. We will see this played out when we cover the resurrections.

Genesis 2:7 "And the Lord God formed man out of the dust of the earth, and breathed into his nostrils the breath of life; and man became a living soul."

This is a very interesting verse. Notice the last two words, living soul. If that dust, which becomes a living soul from God's breath, is not now a separate entity until it dies. How then can it go to heaven as a spirit when dead? Why are the remains in a casket, would we not see it ascend heavenwards at death? The idea of going to heaven when we die is not true; we go to our graves and there we stay 'asleep' resting, totally unconscious until we hear the sound of the trumpet at the Lords coming. This is what I call the 'resurrection call' and the dead in Christ hear it and arise. At this point we become immortal, the breath of God enters our soul and we come alive.

1 Corinthians 15:51-55 "Behold, I show you a mystery; we shall not all sleep, but we shall all be changed. In a moment, in the twinkling of an eye, at the last trumpet; for the trumpet shall sound, and the dead shall be raised incorruptible, and we shall be changed.

For this corruptible must put on in-corruption, and this mortal must put on immortality, then shall be brought to pass the saying that is written; death is swallowed up in victory. O death where is thy sting? O grave, where is they victory?"

In the text above we read of the sleeping, being changed, being raised incorruptible and the last line, questioning the graves hold on the righteous after the resurrection. The big question is how many resurrections are there going to be?

John 3:1-2 "A Pharisee by the name of Nicodemus, a ruler of the Jews, who came to Jesus by night, admitted to Jesus that they knew He had come from God, because no man could do what he did without God being with him. After some discussion, he asked Jesus how this was possible."

In verses 11-13 "Jesus answered him. Verily, verily, I say unto thee, we speak that we do know, and testify that we have seen; and ye receive not our witness. I have told you earthly things, and ye believe not, how shall ye believe heavenly things? And no man has ascended up to heaven, but he that came down from heaven, even the son of man which is in heaven. "

Again I ask the question, how can our loved ones be in heaven?

If you recall how man was formed from the earth in Genesis, then God breathed into his nostrils the breath of life. Well in the book of Ecclesiastes we find out just what happens at the passing away.

Ecclesiastes 12:7 "Then shall the dust return to the earth has it was; and the Spirit (breath) shall return to God who gave it."

So then, how much do our departed dearly beloved know about us, are they here with us?

Ecclesiastes 9:5-6 "For the living know they shall die; but the dead know not anything, neither have they anymore a reward; for the memory of them is forgotten. (They do not remember anything). Also their love, and their hatred, and their envy is now perished; neither have they anymore a portion forever in anything that is done under the sun."

They no longer love, feel, hate or have any part of life. As the text says, they know nothing.

The soul has returned to dust and the spirit (breath) back to God.

Let us see what David and Job have to say on the matter.

Psalms 146:4 "His breath goes forth, he returned to his earth; in that day his thoughts perish."

Job 14:21 "His sons came to honour, and he knows it not; and they are brought low, but he perceived it not of him."

Believe it or not, there are people who will argue this point and try and convince you that it is not true. Their argument is that they have seen or spoken to their loved ones, even both. Remember, the Bible hols only the truth.

We have read of death and sleep which we explained meaning dead or rest. What does Jesus tell his disciples about death?

John 11:14. "These things said he: and after that he said to them. Our friend Lazarus sleeps; but I go, that I may wake him out of his sleep. Then said his disciples, Lord, if he sleeps, he shall do well. How be it Jesus spoke of his death: but they thought he had spoken of his rest in sleep. Then Jesus said unto them plainly, Lazarus is dead."

So, sleep also means dead, but in the broader frame of things, it fits perfectly. We go to the grave to wait the Lords coming and as mentioned in 1 Corinthians 15:51-55 we are changed, but the whole event does not end there, what about the second resurrection?

A question, why did I write this in the book? Because it gave us closure and the assurance, that we would see our son again one day, one beautiful bright morning. It is not all over, kaput, finite because we raised him as a Christian. We know from people that saw him on that sad morning, when he ended his life that he looked peaceful while he sat on the wall talking to God. He always spoke to God, just as we taught him.

Don't give up; you do not know what went through your loved ones mind before they departed. Can you be so sure that your loved one *never* spoke to God? Never quietly contemplated going to church but did not because of pressure from outside? That they never prayed or had religious discussions with friends or colleagues about God and heaven;

you can never be sure, but God knows. Jesus Christ our saviour knows.

Ever wonder where this trouble all started; and why this deception? It is not all that difficult to see, just look around and take note of what is happening. Do I believe in predestination? Yes I do because Jesus predestined us to go to heaven and the devil has predestined us for hell, eternal death. It is our choice which of the two we decide to accept.

So where did this war for our souls begin? Did it begin in our minds, or was it brought on by depression and it is all a matter of mind over matter? No, it is not so simple, it started in a place you and I have never been to before, Heaven.

Revelation 12:7-9 (NIV) 7 "Then war broke out in heaven. Michael and his angels fought against the dragon, and the dragon and his angels fought back".

8 "But he was not strong enough, and they lost their place in heaven."

9 "The great dragon was hurled down— that ancient serpent called the devil, or Satan,

who leads the whole world astray. He was hurled to the earth, and his angels with him."

There you have it, the Devil's plan: lead the world astray from God's word. Deceive them in any way possible; just get them to turn away from God. They more people Satan can lead astray, the greater God's heart aches for the lost; but they do not know it, only Satan and all of heaven knows Gods pain. He sent His son to save us, but lo, we do not read or study His word to find the truth.

The Devil is not a fool, he knows our weaknesses and zeros in on them, be it money, the want of power or fame; he will give it to us just to lead us away from our Heavenly Father. But what is it worth? On a headstone there are two dates; birth and death and between them a dash. That dash is the length of our lives, a short line compared to the age of the earth. What we do in that short space of life will determine eternal life or eternal death. Serve our Heavenly Father of Satan, the father of lies.

Here is what the Bible tell us about the two resurrection. John is in vision and he is shown the end of the world.

New King James Version (NKJV)

Revelation 20-21

Satan Bound 1,000 Years

1"Then I saw an angel coming down from heaven, having the key to the bottomless pit and a great chain in his hand."

2 "He laid hold of the dragon, that serpent of old, who is the Devil and Satan, and bound him for a thousand years;"

3 "And he cast him into the bottomless pit, and shut him up, and set a seal on him, so that he should deceive the nations no more till the thousand years were finished. But after these things he must be released for a little while."

The Saints Reign with Christ 1,000 Years

4 "And I saw thrones, and they sat on them, and judgment was committed to them. Then I saw the souls of those who had been beheaded for their witness to Jesus and for the word of God, who had not worshiped the beast or his image, and had not received his mark on their foreheads or on their hands. And they lived and reigned with Christ for [a]a thousand years."

5 "But the rest of the dead did not live again until the thousand years were finished. This is the first resurrection".

6 "Blessed and holy is he who has part in the first resurrection. Over such the second death has no power, but they shall be priests of God and of Christ, and shall reign with Him a thousand years".

Satanic Rebellion Crushed

7 "Now when the thousand years have expired, Satan will be released from his prison"

8 "and will go out to deceive the nations which are in the four corners of the earth, Gog and Magog, to gather them together to battle, whose number is as the sand of the sea"

9 "They went up on the breadth of the earth and surrounded the camp of the saints and the beloved city. And fire came down from God out of heaven and devoured them."

10 *"The devil, who deceived them, was cast into the lake of fire and brimstone where the beast and the false prophet are. And they will be tormented day and night forever and ever"*

The Great White Throne Judgment

11 *"Then I saw a great white throne and Him who sat on it, from whose face the earth and the heaven fled away. And there was found no place for them".*

12 *"And I saw the dead, small and great, standing before God, and books were opened. And another book was opened, which is the Book of Life. And the dead were judged according to their works, by the things which were written in the books".*

13 *"The sea gave up the dead who were in it, and Death and Hades delivered up the dead who were in them. And they were judged, each one according to his works."*

14 *"Then Death and Hades were cast into the lake of fire. This is the second death."*

15 *"And anyone not found written in the Book of Life was cast into the lake of fire".*

All Things Made New

Revelation 21

1 "I saw a new heaven and a new earth, for the first heaven and the first earth had passed away. Also there was no more sea."

2 "Then I, John, saw the holy city, New Jerusalem, coming down out of heaven from God, prepared as a bride adorned for her husband."

3 "And I heard a loud voice from heaven saying, "Behold, the tabernacle of God is with men, and He will dwell with them, and they shall be His people. God Himself will be with them and be their God."

4 "And God will wipe away every tear from their eyes; there shall be no more death, nor sorrow, nor crying. There shall be no more pain, for the former things have passed away."

5 "Then He who sat on the throne said, "Behold, I make all things new." And He said to me, "Write, for these words are true and faithful."

6 "And He said to me, It is done! I am the Alpha and the Omega, the Beginning and the End.

I will give of the fountain of the water of life freely to him who thirsts."

7 "He who overcomes shall inherit all things, and I will be his God and he shall be My son".

8 "But the cowardly, unbelieving, abominable, murderers, sexually immoral, sorcerers, idolaters, and all liars shall have their part in the lake which burns with fire and brimstone, which is the second death."

The New Jerusalem

9 "Then one of the seven angels who had the seven bowls filled with the seven last plagues came to me and talked with me, saying, Come, I will show you the bride, the Lamb's wife."

10 "And he carried me away in the Spirit to a great and high mountain, and showed me the great city, the holy Jerusalem, descending out of heaven from God,"

11 "having the glory of God. Her light was like a most precious stone, like a jasper stone, clear as crystal".

12 *"Also she had a great and high wall with twelve gates, and twelve angels at the gates, and names written on them, which are the names of the twelve tribes of the children of Israel:"*

13 *"Three gates on the east, three gates on the north, three gates on the south, and three gates on the west".*

14 *"Now the wall of the city had twelve foundations, and on them were the names of the twelve apostles of the Lamb."*

15 *"And he who talked with me had a gold reed to measure the city, its gates, and its wall."*

16 *"The city is laid out as a square; its length is as great as its breadth. And he measured the city with the reed: twelve thousand furlongs. Its length, breadth, and height are equal."*

17 *"Then he measured its wall: one hundred and forty-four cubits, according to the measure of a man, that is, of an angel."*

18 *"The construction of its wall was of jasper; and the city was pure gold, like clear glass."*

19 "The foundations of the wall of the city were adorned with all kinds of precious stones: the first foundation was jasper, the second sapphire, the third chalcedony, the fourth emerald,"

20 "the fifth sardonyx, the sixth sardius, the seventh chrysolite, the eighth beryl, the ninth topaz, the tenth chrysoprase, the eleventh jacinth, and the twelfth amethyst."

21 "The twelve gates were twelve pearls: each individual gate was of one pearl. And the street of the city was pure gold, like transparent glass."

The Glory of the New Jerusalem

22 "But I saw no temple in it, for the Lord God Almighty and the Lamb are its temple."

23 "The city had no need of the sun or of the moon to shine in it, for the glory of God illuminated it. The Lamb is its light."

24 "And the nations]of those who are saved shall walk in its light, and the kings of the earth bring their glory and honour into it."

25 "Its gates shall not be shut at all by day (there shall be no night there)."

26 "And they shall bring the glory and the honour of the nations into it."

27 "But there shall by no means enter it anything that defiles, or causes an abomination or a lie, but only those who are written in the Lamb's Book of Life."

No more lies, deceit, corruption, locked doors, bars on windows, illness, pain, loss or death. Finally, living in harmony with others and being with our Saviour Jesus Christ for eternity. To serve God between two dates is all it takes, try it and win the battle you have been fighting all your life. Give your life over to Jesus and let him take care of you, and introduce him to your family.

I have shared my experience with you in faith that you may have blessed hope should you have to face such devastating news as we did; in the future. The only way to deal with it is through Jesus Christ and His Word. As you have read, I only used Bible texts to back my statements and that from the King James Version. Where I have shared the state of the dead with you is what the Bible, your Bible, teaches, not my ideas or what I think happens after death. May our Father in Heaven, our Saviour Jesus Christ and The Holy Spirit be with you always as you make your decision to follow them and lead your children in their light for their salvation.

Conclusion

A nurse escorted a tired, anxious young man to the bedside of an elderly man. "Your son is here," she whispered to the patient. She had to repeat the words several time before the patient opened his eyes. He was heavily sedated because of his heart attack and he dimly saw the young man standing outside his oxygen tent.

He feebly reached out his hand and the young man tightly wrapped his fingers around it, squeezing a message of encouragement. The nurse brought a chair next to the bedside. All through the night the young man sat holding the old mans hand offering words of hope. The dying man said nothing as he held tightly onto his son. Occasionally lowering his face to caress the old mans hand with his cheek while softly speaking to him.

As dawn approached, the old man died. The young man placed on the bed the lifeless hand he had been holding, and then went to notify the nurse.

While the nurse did what was necessary, the young man waited. When she had finished her task, the nurse began to say words of sympathy to the young man.

But he interrupted her. "Who was that man?" he asked.

The startled nurse replied, "I thought he was your father."

"No, he was not my father," he answered. "I never saw him before in my life."

"Then why didn't you say something when I took you to him?" asked the nurse.

The young man quietly replied, "He needed his son, and his son just wasn't here. When I realised he was too sick to tell whether or not I was his son. That's when I knew how much he needed me...so I became his son."

When Jesus saw how much mankind needed a Savour, He became our Saviour and opened the doors of heaven so that all who believe on him may enter unto Him. He is waiting for you to call on Him.